CALGARY FLAMES CAREER SCORING: 198

NAME	SEASONS	GP	G	A	PTS	PIM
Loob, Hakan	1983-84 to 1988-89	450	193	236	429	189
MacInnis, Al	1981-82 to Present	449	98	319	417	541
MacLellan, B	1988-89	12	2	3	5	14
MacMillan, B	1980-81 to 1981-82	100	32	42	74	61
Macoun, J.	1982-83 to Present	392	45	130	175	457
Marsh, Brad	1980-81 to 1981-82	97	1	13	14	97
McAdam, G.	1981-82	46	12	15	27	18
McCrimmon	1987-88 to Present	152	12	52	64	196
McDonald, L	1981-82 to 1988-89	492	215	191	406	408
McKendry, A	1980-81	36	3	6	9	19
Meredith, G	1980-81 & 1982-83	36	6	4	10	8
Mokosak, C.	1981-82 to 1982-83	42	7	7	14	87
Mullen, Joe	1985-86 to Present	267	154	166	320	71
Murdoch, B.	1980-81 to 1981-82	147	6	36	42	130
Murzyn, D.	1987-88 to Present	104	9	24	33	234
Nattress, Rik	1987-88 to Present	101	3	21	24	84
Nieuwendyk	1986-87 to Present	161	107	73	180	63
Nilsson, K.	1980-81 to 1984-85	345	189	280	469	80
Otto, Joel	1984-85 to Present	298	84	143	227	808
Patterson, C	1983-84 to Present	355	83	96	179	170
Peplinski, J.	1980-81 to Present	699	160	262	422	1452
Plett, Willi	1980-81 to 1981-82	156	59	66	125	527
Priakin, S.	1988-89	2	0	0	0	2
Quinn, Dan	1983-84 to 1986-87	222	72	119	191	100
Ramage, Rob	1987-88 to 1988-89	80	4	19	23	193
Ranheim, P	1988-89	5	0	0	0	0
Rautakallio	1980-81 to 1981-82	156	28	96	124	104
Reierson, D.	1988-89	2	0	0	0	2
Reinhart, P.	1980-81 to 1987-88	438	100	297	397	172
Ribble, Pat	1981-82 to 1982-83	31	0	1	1	20
Riggin, Pat	1980-81 to 1981-82	94	0	0	0	11
Rioux, P.	1982-83	14	1	2	3	4
Risebrough	1982-83 to 1986-87	247	68	101	169	583

NAME	SEASONS	GP	G	A	PTS	PIM
Roberts, G	1986-87 to Present	177	40	41	81	617
Russell, Phil	1980-81 to 1982-83	229	23	66	89	326
Sabourin, K.	1988-89	6	0	1	1	26
Sheehy, Neil	1983-84 to 1987-88	187	12	32	44	606
Smith, Brad	1980-81	45	7	4	11	65
Stiles, Tony	1983-84	30	2	7	9	20
Suter, Gary	1985-86 to Present	286	61	208	269	415
Tambellini, S	1983-84 to 1984-85	120	34	20	54	20
Tonelli, John	1985-86 to 1987-88	161	40	76	116	164
Turnbull, R	1981-82	1	0	0	0	2
Vail, Eric	1980-81 to 1981-82	70	32	37	69	23
Vernon, M.	1982-83 to Present	191	0	14	14	83
Volcan, M.	1983-84	19	1	4	5	18
Walker, H.	1982-83	3	0	0	0	7
Wamsley, R	1987-88 to Present	37	0	1	1	8
Wappel, G.	1980-81 to 1981-82	18	1	1	2	10
Wilson, B.	1980-81	50	5	7	12	94
Wilson, C.	1983-84 to 1987-88	279	84	140	224	113
Wilson, Rik	1985-86	2	0	0	0	0

CALGARY FLAMES CAREER GOALTENDING: 1980-81 to 1988-89

PLAYER	GP	MP	GA	SO	AVG	W	L	T	PCT
Wamsley	37	2,000	100	2	3.00	18	11	4	0.606
Vernon	191	10,492	585	3	3.35	115	49	16	0.683
D'Amour	15	560	32	0	3.43	2	4	2	0.375
Lemelin	303	16,554	1013	6	3.67	136	90	45	0.585
Bouchard	14	760	51	0	4.03	4	5	3	0.458
Riggin	94	5,345	361	2	4.05	10	9	2	0.524
Edwards	114	6,203	420	2	4.06	40	49	13	0.456
Dadswell	27	1,346	99	0	4.41	8	8	3	0.500
Bernhardt	6	280	21	0	4.50	0	5	0	0.000

COUNTDOWN TO THE STANLEY CUP

An Illustrated History of the Calgary Flames

Bob Mummery

POLESTAR
BOOK PUBLISHERS

Countdown to the Stanley Cup:
An Illustrated History of the Calgary Flames

Copyright © 1989 by Bob Mummery

Published in Canada by
Polestar Press Ltd., R.R. 1, Winlaw, B.C., V0G 2J0, 604-226-7670

Distributed in Canada by
Raincoast Book Distribution Ltd., 112 East 3rd Avenue, Vancouver, B.C., V5T 1C8
Phone: 604-873-6581   Fax: 604-874-2711

Printed in Canada

Canadian Cataloguing in Publication Data

Mummery, Bob, 1947 -
ISBN 0-919591-48-5 (pbk.)
1. Calgary Flames (Hockey team) - History.
2. Stanley Cup (Hockey). I. Title.
GV848.C34M84 1989   796.96'26   C89-091542-3

Acknowledgements

The author wishes to thank the following for their help in the development of this book: Brad Watson — contributing photographer, Alberta Report, Jim Brennan, Hockey News, Joyce Mummery, Calgary Herald, Bill McKeown (Westfile), Calgary Sun, Mel Mummery, and Bob Johnson.

The author would especially like to thank the owners, management, players, and staff of the Calgary Flames Hockey Club.

Front Cover photos:

(left to right): Joe Mullen, Lanny McDonald, and Joe Nieuwendyk (see page 120); Doug Risebrough (see page 92); Mike Vernon in goal.

ABOUT THE AUTHOR:

Bob Mummery is an outstanding hockey photographer who has been shooting the Calgary Flames for eight years. Many of his photographs are displayed throughout the Olympic Saddledome. During his career as a professional sports photographer, he has published over four thousand photographs in leading publications, including *Sports Illustrated* and *Time*. *Countdown to the Stanley Cup: An Illustrated History of the Calgary Flames* is Mummery's fourth book. His previous books were *Fuhr On Goaltending*, *Snowbirds: Canada's Ambassadors of the Sky*, and *The Amazing Oilers*. He was born and raised in Minnedosa, Manitoba, and currently lives in Morinville, Alberta, with his wife Joyce and two children.

*To all the fans who have
cheered the Calgary Flames
through the seasons, from
the Corral to the Stanley Cup!*

THE CALGARY FLAMES

RIGHT:
In the Corral, the team had to walk through the lobby to get from their dressing room to the ice.

CALGARY FLAMES OWNERS

Norman N. Green

Harley N. Hotchkiss

Norman L. Kwong

The Calgary Flames owners are a close-knit group of hockey fans. They are: Daryl (Doc) Seaman and his brother, Byron (BJ), who jointly founded Bow Valley Industries Ltd.; oil and gas entrepreneur Harley Hotchkiss; real-estage magnate Norman Green; Sonia Scurfield, who took responsibility for her husband Ralph's share of the club when he died in 1985; and Norman Kwong, president and general manager of the Calgary Stampeder Football Club.

"We looked upon it as a community project from the start." These words from "Doc" Seaman sum up the principles upon which the six owners govern their hockey team. They are dedicated to community involvement and have a strong commitment to the game of hockey.

6

CALGARY FLAMES OWNERS

Sonia Scurfield

Byron J. Seaman

Daryl K. (Doc) Seaman

For the Seamans, it was their wish to participate in a program that would return hockey to the basics they once knew that led them to become involved in the NHL franchise for the City of Calgary. An NHL team located in Calgary would serve a variety of purposes: it would insure a primary tenant for a new hockey arena; it would help Calgary in its Olympic bid; the building could house a research centre; the arena could become home to a National Team which would enjoy the support of the team; it would initiate an important rivalry that would help insure the success of both NHL teams in Alberta; and it would put Calgary on the hockey map — and, after the Olympics, on the world map — and establish the foundation for a future Stanley Cup champion.

BRINGING THE FLAMES TO CALGARY

1979-80 ATLANTA FLAMES

The year was 1979. Thomas Cousins, owner of the NHL's Atlanta Flames, had hung out the "For Sale" sign. The previous seven seasons had definitely been a struggle for his expansion team. Atlanta was ultimately proving that it wasn't a hotbed of hockey. Despite an impressive new 15,000 seat arena, The Omni, the team had started to run into tough times in Year Four. And, in the eight seasons the club operated as the Atlanta Flames, they failed to advance past the first round of the playoffs.

Attendance fell off to the point where the franchise was losing close to a million dollars annually. Discussions had taken place with interested groups in both Dallas and Houston, but that was as far as it went. The Seaman brothers of Calgary arranged a number of meetings with Cousins. By March of 1980, a deal was nearing completion when Nelson Skalbania, a high-flying Vancouver businessman, stepped in. With a last minute offer, submitted on a cocktail napkin, Skalbania purchased the Atlanta Flames. This came as somewhat of a shock to the Calgarians who had been following every step in the negoti-

ations, but nevertheless, an NHL hockey team was headed their way.

Almost immediately, Skalbania sold a fifty percent interest in the team to Byron and Daryl Seaman and their group of Calgary businessmen: Ralph Scurfield, Norman Green, Harley Hotchkiss, and Norman Kwong. The official announcement was May 21, 1980. Within 16 months, Nelson Skalbania sold his remaining interest in the team to his partners and the Flames were now completely Calgary owned.

For months, Calgary had been alive with rumours of the sale, and when it was finally announced, the fans were ecstatic. They scurried to find out anything and everything about Atlanta's roster. The fans found the Flames had strong and aggressive forwards such as Willi Plett and Ken Houston. The offence would centre around skilled players like forty-goal scorer Kent Nilsson, right winger Bob MacMillan, and centre Guy Chouinard. They were also strong in goal with proven NHL goaltenders Pat Riggin and Dan Bouchard. And talented defenceman Paul Reinhart, only in his second year, held great promise for the future.

The Flames would play in the Stampede Corral, which couldn't compete with the established rinks around the NHL. However, with the promise of a world class facility to be built for the Olympics in 1988 — one that would eventually be capable of seating 20,000 spectators — the Corral would do for a start.

Approximately 6,700 people could fit into the Corral, with a further 700 standing room tickets. Unfortunately, because of the small seating capacity, the cost of a season ticket would be the highest in the league. Nelson Skalbania remarked that if anyone brought their money down to the Corral on the weekend, the Flames would accept it. There was no hesitation on the part of the fans. Tickets were sold out immediately. By Monday morning it was total chaos. Seven hundred boxes, approximately fourteen inches square, were painted on the cement floor and sold as season ticket standing room. And separate A and B packages were arranged that split season's tickets, enabled more people to attend games, and helped to establish a broader season ticket base. A week later at a press conference everyone was notified that the season ticket campaign scheduled to start the next day had been cancelled because all the tickets had been sold!

The Corral was packed for the Flames opening night game against the Quebec Nordiques, and every seat in the arena was filled for the next three seasons. A Flames ticket became the most sought after and difficult to obtain in the entire National Hockey League.

SEC. **N** ROW **1** SEAT **69**

RESERVED SEAT $21.00

GAME 1

THURSDAY
7:30 P.M.
OCT. 9, 1980

CALGARY
VS.
QUEBEC
STAMPEDE CORRAL

GAME 1

THURSDAY
7:30 P.M.
OCT. 9, 1980

1980 - 81 SEASON

N **1** **69**
SEC. ROW SEAT

Bill Clement (10), Paul Reinhart (23) and goaltender Pat Riggin.

1980-81

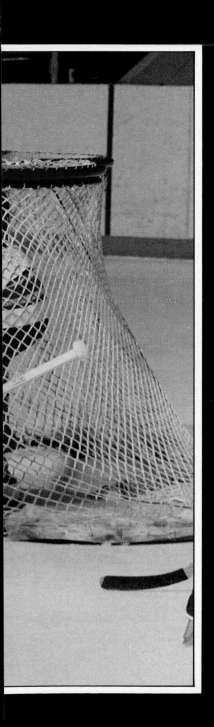

*T*he new owners of the Flames were astute business leaders who recognized a good organization when they saw one. They decided to keep intact the existing management team consisting of General Manager Cliff Fletcher, Assistant General Manager David Poile, and Coach Al MacNeil. Cliff Fletcher is the first, and only, general manager the Flames organization has ever had, both in Atlanta and Calgary. Fletcher started off as a scout in the Montreal Canadiens organization and spent ten years there under the influence of Sam Pollack. When the St. Louis Blues joined the NHL in 1967, Fletcher became their eastern Canadian scout. Two years later, he was named their Assistant General Manager. He spent the next four years with the team, during which time the Blues never missed the playoffs. Three of those four years St. Louis was in the Stanley Cup finals. In 1972, the NHL expanded again, and Cliff Fletcher was appointed General Manager of the new Atlanta Flames. In his seventeen-year-career as both general manager and president, his teams have missed the playoffs only twice.

In his first season in Calgary, however, the team's tremendous success, both on and off the ice, was a surprise even for him. In their inaugural season in Calgary, the Flames set no less than sixteen team records. They amassed their highest points total ever with 92. At home in the feared Stampede Corral, they won 25 games and lost only 5, with 10 ties. They scored 198 goals at home — almost five per game — with 81 of those coming on the power play. Kent Nilsson had shown his touch by amassing an incredible 131 points (including 49 goals), still a team record to this day. Big Willi Plett stood his, and his teammates' ground, accumulating 239 penalty minutes, and in the playoffs he again came through by scoring eight goals, while Guy Chouinard led all Flames in playoff scoring with 17 points.

In goal, Pat Riggin held down the majority of work, playing in 42 games, while newly-acquired Reggie Lemelin had 14 wins against only six losses and seven ties. Dan Bouchard, traded early in the season to Quebec, played in 14 games. With their 92 total points, the Flames placed seventh overall in the league in their first season in Calgary.

Defenceman Phil Russell starts a rush while goaltender Pat Riggin looks on.

CALGARY FLAMES

GAME #1

This Certifies That _____
    Was In Attendance For The First
    Calgary Flames Regular Season Game
    In The National Hockey League
    On Thursday, October 9, 1980
    At The Stampede Corral
    Calgary Flames vs. Quebec Nordiques

Score: Calgary ____ Quebec ____

Cliff Fletcher
Cliff Fletcher
General Manager

A true collector's item. Fewer than 8,000 Calgarians can claim ownership of one of these certificates handed out by the Calgary Flames on their opening night. The game, played against the Quebec Nordiques, ended in a 5-5 tie.

"Reflecting on our first year here, it was a very successful season. With the high boards in the Corral, and the crowds adding another form of intimidation, our players got caught up in it. We had a winning and successful year."

Cliff Fletcher

Opening night at the Corral, October 9th, 1980. Calgarian and former President of the NHL, and a member of the Hockey Hall of Fame, Merv Dutton, is greeted at centre ice by Mayor Ross Alger. Just behind Mr. Dutton is NHL President John Ziegler, followed by then Flames' majority owner Nelson Skalbania.

The clock in the Stampede Corral signals the end of the first Flames regular season game played on home ice. Calgary and the Quebec Nordiques tied 5-5.

PLAYOFFS

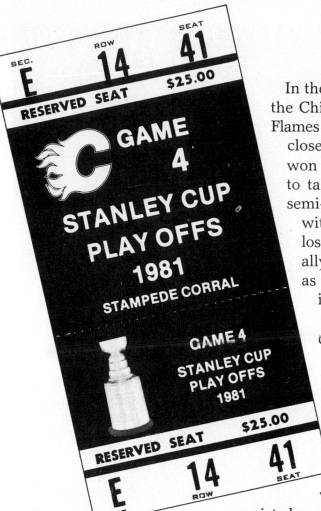

In the first round of the playoffs, the Flames defeated the Chicago Black Hawks in three straight games. The Flames then met the Philadelphia Flyers. In an extremely close series that went the full seven games, Calgary won the seventh and deciding game at Philadelphia to take the series and move on to the Stanley Cup semi-finals. Playing a hot Minnesota North Stars team with a high-flying Bobby Smith at centre, Calgary lost the series four games to two. Minnesota eventually lost out to the New York Islanders in the finals, as the Islanders went on to their second Cup win in a row.

All things considered, it had been a very successful start for the Flames in Calgary. As hockey fever had become an integral part of Calgary society, a pride in their team had arisen that would never wane. A trip to the Stanley Cup semi-finals in the first year of their existence was more than anyone had dared to dream.

That season had also seen the emergence of Paul Reinhart, the rookie defenceman who set new Flames standards for both goals and assists by a defenceman. He had established himself as one of the NHL's premier point men on the power play, quickly gaining the respect of every penalty killing unit in the NHL. Willi Plett, while leading the team in penalty minutes served, also contributed in an unexpected fashion by scoring 38 goals, his best season ever. These two factors led him to quickly become the most popular player on the team. During that initial season, a total of 33 different players had worn the Flames colours, and the Flames had established to their fans, and the rest of the NHL, that bench strength was something that they would not have to worry about in the foreseeable future.

FAR LEFT:
Guy Chouinard and Paul Reinhart.

LEFT:
Willi Plett scores series-winning goal against Tony Esposito in overtime playoff action against the Chicago Black Hawks.

Kent Nilsson set a team record that still stands for total points by scoring 49 goals and 82 assists for 131 points. Nilsson was third in overall NHL scoring, and Calgury's first Molson Cup winner.

1980-81 CALGARY FLAMES

THIRD ROW: Pekka Rautakallio, Bob Murdoch, Paul Reinhart, Jim Peplinski, Willi Plett, Phil Russell, Burt Wilson, Jamie Hislop.

SECOND ROW: Bobby Stewart (Equipment Manager), Dan Labraaten, Kevin LaVallee, Randy Holt, Kent Nilsson, Eric Vail, Guy Chouinard, Don Lever, Bob MacMillan, Jim Murray (Trainer).

FIRST ROW: Rejean Lemelin, Bill Clement, Al MacNeil (Coach), Cliff Fletcher (General Manager), Brad Marsh (Captain), David Poile (Assistant General Manager), Pierre Page (Assistant Coach), Ken Houston, Pal Riggin.

STATS

CALGARY FLAMES

REGULAR SEASON HIGHLIGHTS

Most Points
KENT NILSSON 131 *

Most Goals
KENT NILSSON 49

Most Assists
KENT NILSSON 82 *

Most Penalty Minutes
WILLI PLETT 239

Most Wins Goalie
PAT RIGGIN 21

Molson Cup
KENT NILSSON

* Flame Record

PLAYOFF HIGHLIGHTS

Most Points
GUY CHOUINARD 17

Most Goals
BOB MacMILLAN 8
WILLI PLETT 8

Most Assists
GUY CHOUINARD 14
PAUL REINHART 14

Most Penalty Minutes
WILLI PLETT 89

Most Wins Goalie
PAT RIGGIN 6

Overtime Goals
WILLI PLETT 1

Centre Bill Clement played 78 games in the 1980-81 season, scoring 12 goals and 20 assists for 32 points.

STATS

1980-81

Coach		REGULAR SEASON								PLAYOFFS				
	GP	W	L	T	PTS	GF	GA		GP	W	L	GF	GA
Al MacNeil	80	39	27	14	92	329	298		16	9	7	56	60

Left winger Don Lever carries the puck into the Philadelphia zone during the playoffs. The Flames won the series, four games to three.

STATISTICS — REGULAR SEASON

PLAYER		GP	G	A	PTS	PIM
Kent Nilsson		80	49	*82	*131	26
Guy Chouinard		52	31	52	83	24
Willi Plett		78	38	30	68	239
Paul Reinhart		74	18	49	67	52
Eric Vail		64	28	36	64	23
Bob MacMillan		77	28	35	63	47
Don Lever		62	26	31	57	56
Jamie Hislop	Que.	50	19	22	41	15
	Cal.	29	6	9	15	11
	Tot.	79	25	31	56	26
Pekka Rautakallio		76	11	45	56	64
Jim Peplinski		80	13	25	38	108
Kevin LaVallee		76	15	20	35	16
Bill Clement		78	12	20	32	33
Ken Houston		42	15	15	30	93
Phil Russell		80	6	23	29	104
Dan Labraaten	Det.	44	3	8	11	12
	Cal.	27	9	7	16	13
	Tot.	71	12	15	27	25
Bob Murdoch		74	3	19	22	54
Brad Marsh		80	1	12	13	87
Bert Wilson		50	5	7	12	94
Brad Smith		45	7	4	11	65
Alex McKendry		36	3	6	9	19
Earl Ingarfield		16	2	3	5	6
Denis Cyr		10	1	4	5	0
Randy Holt		48	0	5	5	165
Dan Bouchard		14	0	4	4	6
Dave Hindmarch		1	1	0	1	0
Greg Meredith		3	1	0	1	0
Mike Dwyer		4	0	1	1	4
Gord Wappel		7	0	1	1	4
Rejean Lemelin		29	0	1	1	2
Pat Riggin		42	0	1	1	7
Tony Curtale		2	0	0	0	0
Bob Gould		3	0	0	0	0
Steve Konroyd		4	0	0	0	4
* Flame Record	**Totals**	80	329	547	876	1426

GOALTENDERS	GP	MP	GA	AVG	W	L	T
Rejean Lemelin	29	1629	88	3.24	14	6	7
Pat Riggin	42	2411	154	3.83	21	16	4
Dan Bouchard	14	760	51	4.03	4	5	3
Totals		4800	298	3.73	39	27	14

ENG: Lemelin (2), Riggin (3)
SO: Lemelin (2)

Guy Chouinard (16), Captain Phil Russell (5), Charlie Bourgeois (2) and goaltender Pat Riggin. (Inset) Coach Al MacNeil and Assistant Coach Pierre Page.

1981-82

Shortly after the end of the first season there was an ownership and management change. Nelson Skalbania sold his majority interest to the other six owners and Cliff Fletcher was appointed President and General Manager. When the second season started defenceman Bob Murdoch, an eleven-year NHL veteran, was appointed playing coach, working with fellow assistant coach Pierre Page and coach Al MacNeil.

In another off-season move, the Flames signed a mobile puck-handling Finn, Kari Eloranta, to their defensive corps, joining countryman Pekka Rauta-kallio. But other than shoring up their defence, the Flames would enter the new season with virtually the same team that had taken them all the way to the Stanley Cup semi-finals the year before. Expected to win their division, the Flames lost eight of their

first ten games. This would prove to be a year of change.

The captaincy became the first of many changes. Within the first month, Phil Russell became the new captain when Brad Marsh was dealt to Philadelphia. In return, Calgary got versatile Mel Bridgman, the former Flyer captain. But it wasn't too long before President and General Manager Cliff Fletcher was consummating a major acquisition — Lanny McDonald was coming to town. The November trade saw Bobby MacMillan and Don Lever go to the Colorado Rockies in exchange for the goal-scoring right winger from Hanna. It would turn out to be one of the most astute, and most popular, trades that Cliff Fletcher had ever made.

Injuries played a large part in Calgary's low season total of 75 points. Kent Nilsson missed half of the season with a separated shoulder and fell to 55 points from his previous year's record 131 points. Guy Chouinard was sidelined for a total of sixteen games, and the newly acquired Lanny McDonald also missed several games due to a variety of

Bob Murdoch helped to give the Flames solid defence as well as assist in his dual job as assistant coach.

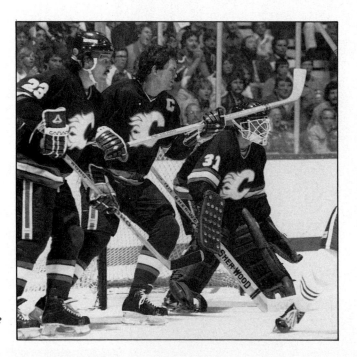

Paul Reinhart, captain Phil Russell, and goalie Reggie Lemelin were an awesome defensive threesome.

injuries. Even so, in 55 games played, he scored a team-leading 34 goals, for a total of 67 points as a Flame. And high-scoring defenceman Paul Reinhart was forced to sit out eighteen games due to an ankle injury.

During the season, three players were called up from Calgary's Central Hockey League affiliate in Oklahoma City — defencemen Charlie Bourgeois and Steve Konroyd, and right winger Denis Cyr, Calgary's 1980 first round draft pick. Another trade saw Randy Holt and Bob Gould sent to Washington in exchange for defenceman Pat Ribble.

Rugged centre Jim Peplinski was a bright note throughout the season, scoring 30 goals and establishing himself as one of the team leaders. A name unfamiliar to fans would show up in the game summaries that year. Called up from Oklahoma City for two games, this native Calgarian registered no points but did amass a total of nine penalty minutes. His name was Tim Hunter.

It had been a bit of a dismal year overall, but change was on the horizon. Things would only get better.

Rugged crowd pleaser Jim Peplinski more than doubled his goal output to 30 in his second full season as a Flame.

Newly acquired Mel Bridgman played 63 games for Calgary after coming from Philadelphia, and led the team in scoring with 87 points.

Calgary's first key acquisition was Lanny McDonald. On November 25, 1981, McDonald came from the Colorado Rockies in exchange for Don Lever and Bobby MacMillan. Adding McDonald to their roster brought two key ingredients to the team — credibility and respectability. Having already played six-and-a-half seasons with the Toronto Maple Leafs and two-and-a half with Colorado, his experience and leadership qualities showed themselves on and off the ice immediately. In his first season with the Flames, he would play in 55 games, scoring 34 goals and adding 33 assists for 67 points. Combined with the six goals scored at the start of the season while still in a Rockies' uniform, he would lead the Flames in goals scored with 40.

Pat Riggin, the 1981-82 Molson Cup winner, played in 52 games.

1981 - 82 CALGARY FLAMES

THIRD ROW: Paul Reinhart, Mel Bridgman, Steve Konroyd, Pat Ribble, Ken Houston, Willi Plett, Jim Peplinski, Charles Bourgeois, Eddy Beers, Lanny McDonald, Dan Labraaten.

SECOND ROW: Kevin LaVallee, Guy Chouinard, Bill Clement, Gary McAdam, Phil Russell (Captain), Bob Murdoch (Assistant Coach), Pekka Rautakallio, Jamie Hislop, Denis Cyr, Kent Nilsson.

FIRST ROW: Jim Murray (Trainer), Rejean Lemelin, Al MacNeil (Coach), David Poile (Assistant General Manager), Norman Kwong (Owner), Byron Seaman (Owner), Cliff Fletcher (President and General Manager), Harley Hotchkiss (Owner), Ralph Scurfield (Owner), Norman Green (Owner), Pierre Page (Assistant Coach), Pat Riggin, Bobby Stewart (Equipment Manager).

PLAYOFFS
CALGARY VS. VANCOUVER

Paul Reinhart

Mel Bridgman and Willi Plett

The Flames finished the regular season in third place in the Smythe Division, two points behind the Vancouver Canucks. Calgary's 75 points placed them twelfth overall in the league. Entering the playoffs, with Vancouver holding home ice advantage, they lost both games to the surging Canucks, with the second game being decided in overtime. Returning home to the Corral, they were eliminated by Vancouver, who eventually went all the way to the Stanley Cup finals before losing to the New York Islanders.

STATS

1981 - 82

	REGULAR SEASON							PLAYOFFS				
Coach	GP	W	L	T	PTS	GF	GA	GP	W	L	GF	GA
Al MacNeil	80	29	34	17	75	334	345	3	0	3	5	10

REGULAR SEASON HIGHLIGHTS

Most Points
MEL BRIDGMAN 87
(Calgary 75, Philadelphia 12)

Most Goals
LANNY McDONALD 40
(Calgary 34, Colorado 6)

Most Assists
GUY CHOUINARD 57

Most Penalty Minutes
WILLI PLETT 288

Most Wins Goalie
PAT RIGGIN 19

Molson Cup
PAT RIGGIN

PLAYOFF HIGHLIGHTS

Most Points
KENT NILSSON 3
WILLI PLETT 3

Most Goals
MEL BRIDGMAN 2

Most Assists
KENT NILSSON 3

Most Penalty Minutes
WILLI PLETT 39

STATISTICS — REGULAR SEASON

PLAYER		GP	G	A	PTS	PIM
Mel Bridgman	Cal.	63	26	49	75	94
	Pha.	9	7	5	12	47
	Tot.	72	33	54	87	141
Lanny McDonald	Cal.	55	34	33	67	37
	Col.	16	6	9	15	20
	Tot.	71	40	42	82	57
Guy Chouinard		64	23	57	80	12
Pekka Rautakallio		80	17	51	68	40
Jim Peplinski		74	30	37	67	115
Kevin LaVallee		76	32	29	61	30
Paul Reinhart		62	13	48	61	17
Willi Plett		78	21	36	57	288
Kent Nilsson		41	26	29	55	8
Ken Houston		70	22	22	44	91
Jamie Hislop		80	16	25	41	35
Phil Russell		71	4	25	29	110
Gary McAdam		46	12	15	27	18
Denis Cyr		45	12	10	22	13
Dan Labraaten		43	10	12	22	6
Bob Murdoch		73	3	17	20	76
Don Lever		23	8	11	19	6
Steve Konroyd		63	3	14	17	78
Bill Clement		69	4	12	16	28
Charles Bourgeois		54	2	13	15	112
Bob MacMillan		23	4	7	11	14
Eric Vail		6	4	1	5	0
Kari Eloranta		16	0	5	5	14
Pat Riggin		52	0	5	5	4
Dave Hindmarch		6	3	0	3	0
Bob Gould		16	3	0	3	4
Pat Ribble	Was.	12	1	2	3	14
	Cal.	3	0	0	0	2
	Tot.	15	1	2	3	16
Eddy Beers		5	1	1	2	21
Mike Dwyer		5	0	2	2	0
Gord Wappel		11	1	0	1	6
Carl Mokosak		1	0	1	1	0
Brad Marsh		17	0	1	1	10
Rejean Lemelin		34	0	1	1	0
Al MacInnis		1	0	0	0	0
Randy Turnbull		1	0	0	0	2
Bruce Eakin		1	0	0	0	0
Bobby Lalonde		1	0	0	0	0
Tim Hunter		2	0	0	0	9
Randy Holt		8	0	0	0	9
Totals		80	334	569	903	1291

GOALTENDERS	GP	MP	GA	AVG	W	L	T
Pat Riggin	52	2934	207	4.23	19	19	11
Rejean Lemelin	34	1866	135	4.34	10	15	6
Totals		4800	342	4.28	29	34	17

ENG: Riggin, Lemelin (2)
SO: Riggin (2)

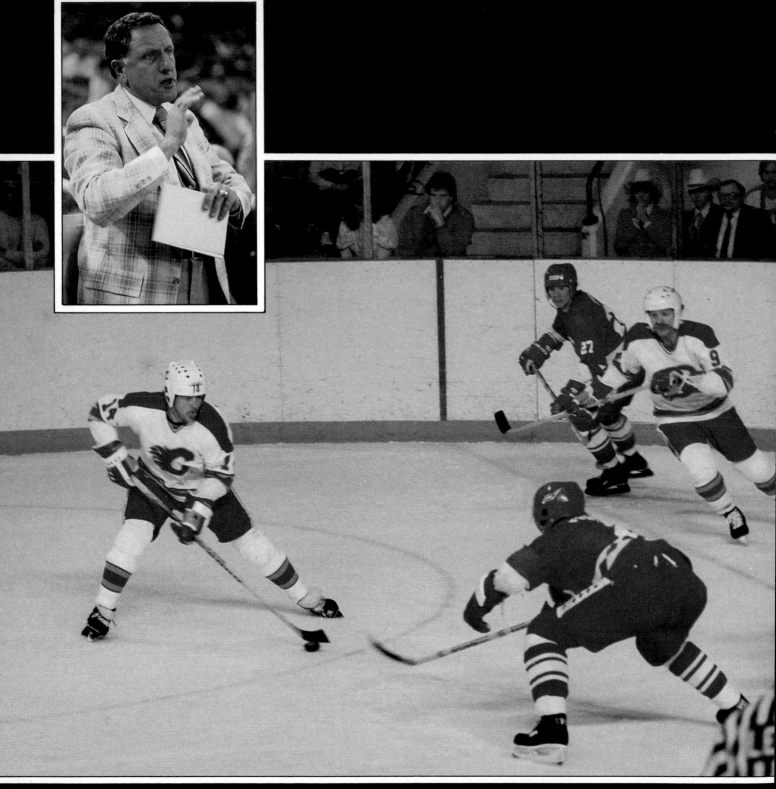

Kent Nilsson, Lanny McDonald and Paul Reinhart in a game against Moscow Dynamo. (Inset) Coach Bob Johnson.

1982-83

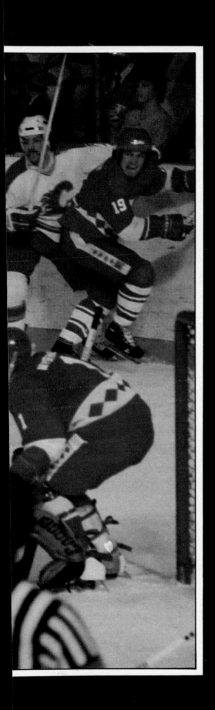

Bob Johnson's success in coaching the U.S. team in the 1981 Canada Cup had attracted the attention of the NHL. Cliff Fletcher had been one of the General Managers who followed Bob Johnson's success and was impressed enough to approach him in Finland during a subsequent World Championship. Fletcher had two questions for Bob Johnson. "Can you work for me?" and "Would you live in Canada?" The answer to both questions was "yes."

Johnson had been approached by other teams, but from the standpoint of getting in on the ground floor of rebuilding a team, of playing in a new world-class hockey facility, plus the excitement of the Edmonton-Calgary rivalry, he knew this would be the best situation. Coach Johnson became a Flame.

Calgary's arch rivals to the north, the Edmonton Oilers, had finished the previous season with 113 points, 38 points ahead of the Flames. No matter

Steve Konroyd, a second-round 1980 draft pick, was solid on defence.

how well the Flames would do, they would always be compared to the Oilers. The fact that the Oilers had also been upset in the first playoff round was of no consequence. Changes had to be made.

The first, and biggest, change happened before the June draft in Montreal when Bob Johnson was made coach, and Al MacNeil became the new assistant general manager. Johnson, then 51 years old, had won three National Collegiate Athletic Association championships. He took the Wisconsin Badgers to the top first in 1973, again in 1977, and finally in 1981, during which time his teams compiled 367 wins, 175 losses and 23 ties in a fifteen-year span. Some of his players that had graduated to the NHL included Craig Norwich of the Jets, Brian Engblom of the Canadiens, Wayne Thomas of the Rangers, and Mike Eaves and Mark Johnson (the coach's son) of the North Stars. Later graduates included Chris Chelios (Canadiens) and future Flame Rookie-of-the-Year, Gary Suter.

In other management moves, David Poile, formerly assistant general manager, had moved on to become general manager of the Washington Capitals. Pierre Page, former assistant coach under Al MacNeil, was named coach and general manager of Calgary's farm team in Colorado. And playing coach Bob Murdoch finally hung up his skates to become the full-time assistant coach under Bob Johnson.

In off-season trades, President and General Manager Cliff Fletcher had been quick to move. Pat Riggin was dealt to the Washington Capitals, while Don Edwards and Richie Dunn were acquired from the Buffalo Sabres. And Willi Plett was traded to the Minnesota North Stars. Just before training camp opened, Fletcher made another major acquisition. He managed to pry tenacious centre Doug Risebrough from Montreal, where he had played on five Stanley Cup winners. And Fletcher got another centre in November, getting Carey Wilson from Chicago in exchange for Denis Cyr.

The Flames opened the season at the Northlands Coliseum in Edmonton. Newcomer Don Edwards started in goal and the Flames started the season just as they had ended the last. They lost 7-5 to the Oilers, then 5-4 to the New York Islanders, and 3-1 to the Los Angeles Kings. It was the fourth game of the season before the first win, but it came with a bang. A resounding 9-4 victory over the Oilers. And that was followed two nights later with a 6-4 win over the Detroit Red Wings. The season was underway and Badger Bob, notebook firmly in hand, had chalked up his first two NHL victories.

Bob Johnson on Doug Risebrough:
"I wanted Doug Risebrough on my team. He was a competitor, and I had seen and heard nothing but good things about him. He was a character player who gave inspiration to everyone around him. I was very happy when we got Risebrough."

The story of the season, however, was Lanny McDonald. In his first complete season with Calgary, he played in all 80 games, scoring goals at an amazing pace. And when it was over he had popped in an incredible 66 goals. To that time, only three players in NHL history — Wayne Gretzky, Phil Esposito, and Mike Bossy — had scored more goals in one season. The City of Calgary went wild as McDonald played his best season ever, though Kent Nilsson rebounded from injuries to lead the team in total points with 104. Guy Chouinard led the team in assists with 59, while Don Edwards and Reggie Lemelin had 16 wins each in the nets.

Overall, the season was marginally better than the previous year, as the Flames recorded 32 wins, 34 losses, and 14 ties — three points ahead of last year. They again placed twelfth in the league, but moved up to second overall in the Smythe, giving them home-ice advantage over the third-place Canucks in the playoffs.

For Bob Johnson, the turning point in his first season was the exhibition game played against the Russians. The national Soviet team had beaten both Montreal and Quebec and was having great success until it was stopped 3-2 in the Corral. That win helped turn the season around for the Flames.

But there would be changes. Management decided that one of the best ways to improve would be via the free agent route — and Calgary was uniquely situated to take full advantage. Firstly, Bob Johnson had fifteen years of experience coaching in the U.S. college system and knew the high quality of some of the players in the ranks. Secondly, Cliff Fletcher had enlarged the scouting staff which meant more comprehensive coverage could now be given to college games. The free agent signings began and eventually totalled eleven players before a change in rules closed the door. During the next three years, Johnson's team of free agents, players acquired in trades, and late round draft picks would mature and meld together.

RIGHT:

Lanny McDonald, the Hanna Sniper, scored 66 goals during the 1982-83 season. In accomplishing that feat, he joined the ranks of only three players who had (to that date) scored 66 or more goals in regular season play: Phil Esposito, Mike Bossy, and Wayne Gretzky.

BELOW:

Mel Bridgman, acquired from the Philadelphia Flyers in 1981, was a strong two-way player at both centre and left wing.

1982- 83 CALGARY FLAMES

FOURTH ROW: Tim Harrer, Greg Meredith, Jim Peplinski, Charles Bourgeois, Steve Konroyd, Tim Hunter, Ed Beers, Kari Jalonen, Pat Ribble.

THIRD ROW: Kari Eloranta, Dave Hindmarch, Kent Nilsson, Lanny McDonald, Steve Christoff, Paul Reinhart, Richie Dunn, Mel Bridgman.

SECOND ROW: Bobby Stewart (Equipment Manager), Doug Riscbrough, Denis Cyr, Kevin LaVallee, Bobby Francis, Jamie Hislop, Bruce Eakin, Guy Chouinard, Jim Murray (Trainer).

FRONT ROW: (left to right) Don Edwards, Rejean Lemelin, Bob Murdoch (Assistant Coach), Al Coates (Assistant to President & P.R. Director), Cliff Fletcher (President and General Manager), Bob Johnson (Coach), Phil Russell (Captain), Tim Bernhardt.

PLAYOFFS

During the regular season, the Flames had beaten the Canucks five times, with only two losses. Calgary was anxious to avenge last year's first round playoff loss. In the Corral, Calgary came out strong, winning the first two games. In Vancouver, they dropped the third game of the series 5-4, but won in overtime in game four, 4-3, to move on to round two in the playoffs. The stage was set. The Battle of Alberta was about to begin.

The Smythe Division final opened in Edmonton on April 14, 1983. The Oilers took full advantage of home-ice, winning the first game 6-3, the second 5-1. Then the series switched to the Stampede Corral for the last NHL series ever to be played in that building.

In game three, Edmonton scored three short-handed goals on the way to a 10-2 triumph. Calgary rebounded in game four with a 6-5 win. But two nights later the series ended in Edmonton with the Oilers winning 9-1.

There were many bright spots during the year, however, including Lanny McDonald's team record 66 goals, Risebrough's leadership, and the strong play of Nilsson and Reinhart. As for the future, well, there was a hometown kid, Mike Vernon, who looked good in goal for the Wranglers. And, across the street, an army of workmen were rushing to complete the new home of the Flames — the Olympic Saddledome.

TOP:
Ralph Scurfield and Peter Pocklington enjoy watching their teams in the first "Battle of Alberta."

MIDDLE:
Doug Risebrough

BOTTOM:
Saddledome under construction.

36

STATS

1982 - 83

	REGULAR SEASON							PLAYOFFS				
Coach	GP	W	L	T	PTS	GF	GA	GP	W	L	GF	GA
Bob Johnson	80	32	34	14	78	321	317	9	4	5	30	49

REGULAR SEASON HIGHLIGHTS

Most Points
KENT NILSSON 104

Most Goals
LANNY McDONALD 66 *

Most Assists
GUY CHOUINARD 59

Most Penalty Minutes
DOUG RISEBROUGH 138

Most Wins Goalie
REJEAN LEMELIN 16
DON EDWARDS 16

Trophies - Awards
NHL 2nd Team All-Star RW
Masterton Trophy
Molson Cup
LANNY McDONALD

* Flame Record

PLAYOFF HIGHLIGHTS

Most Points
KENT NILSSON 12

Most Goals
PAUL REINHART 6

Most Assists
KENT NILSSON 11

Most Penalty Minutes
TIM HUNTER 70

Most Wins Goalie
REJEAN LEMELIN 3

Overtime Goals
EDDY BEERS 1
GREG MEREDITH 1

STATISTICS — REGULAR SEASON

PLAYER	GP	G	A	PTS	PIM
Kent Nilsson	80	46	58	104	10
Lanny McDonald	80	*66	32	98	90
Paul Reinhart	78	17	58	75	28
Guy Chouinard	80	13	59	72	18
Doug Risebrough	71	21	37	58	138
Mel Bridgman	79	19	31	50	103
Kari Eloranta	80	4	40	44	43
Jim Peplinski	80	15	26	41	134
Kevin LaVallee	60	19	16	35	17
Jamie Hislop	79	14	19	33	17
Phil Russell	78	13	18	31	112
Eddy Beers	41	11	15	26	21
Dave Hindmarch	60	11	12	23	23
Jim Jackson	48	8	12	20	7
Steve Christoff	45	9	8	17	4
Steve Konroyd	79	4	13	17	73
Richie Dunn	80	3	11	14	47
Carl Mokosak	41	7	6	13	87
Kari Jalonen	25	9	3	12	4
Greg Meredith	35	5	4	9	28
Charles Bourgeois	15	2	3	5	21
Jamie Macoun	22	1	4	5	25
Rejean Lemelin	39	0	5	5	7
Al MacInnis	14	1	3	4	9
Pierre Rioux	14	1	2	3	4
Denis Cyr	11	1	1	2	0
Tim Hunter	16	1	0	1	54
Pat Ribble	28	0	1	1	18
Don Edwards	39	0	1	1	0
Mike Vernon	2	0	0	0	0
Howard Walker	3	0	0	0	7
Tim Harrer	3	0	0	0	2
Gord Hampson	4	0	0	0	5
Tim Bernhardt	6	0	0	0	0
Totals	80	321	466	819	1156

*New Flames' Record

GOALTENDERS	GP	MP	GA	AVG	W	L	T
Rejean Lemelin	39	2211	133	3.61	16	12	8
Don Edwards	39	2209	148	4.02	16	15	6
Tim Bernhardt	6	280	21	4.50	0	5	0
Mike Vernon	2	100	11	6.60	0	2	0
Totals		4800	313	3.91	32	34	14

ENG: Lemelin (3), Edwards
SO: Edwards

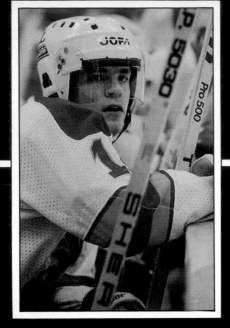

(Inset) Hakan Loob

1983-84

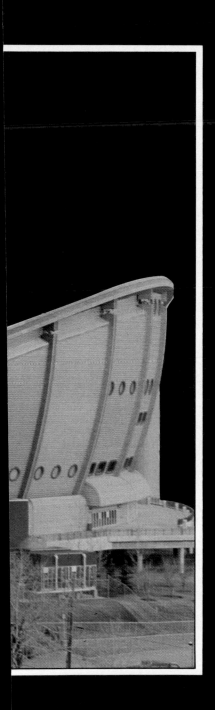

*T*here was no question about it. It was the best entertainment facility in all of North America. The Olympic Saddledome, adjacent to the Stampede Corral, would initially seat 16,605 for the Flames home games. That would amount to over eight thousand new fans. But there were other reasons for excitement about the Flames. Once again, Cliff Fletcher had been busy in the off-season. Though it wasn't totally apparent at the time, within a couple of seasons it would be talked of as, ''the great free agent rout.''

Right wing Colin Patterson had been signed as a free agent at the end of the previous season, then, in August, defencemen Paul Baxter and Neil Sheehy became Flames. In trades in the off-season, Steve Bozek was acquired from Los Angeles in exchange for Kevin LaVallee and Carl Mokosak, and Mike

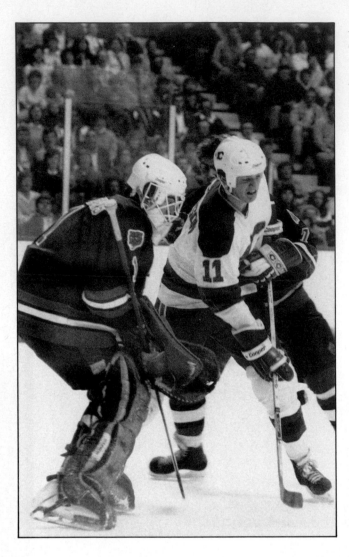

Free agent Colin Patterson gave the Flames the big, strong defensive-minded forward they'd been looking for. He was the team's top plus-minus player at plus 17, and was prominent on the checking line with veteran Doug Risebrough and rookie Richard Kromm.

Eaves came from the Minnesota North Stars in exchange for a future draft choice. Fletcher also got centre Steve Tambellini, plus Joel Quenneville from New Jersey for Mel Bridgman and Phil Russell. In July, Quenneville and Richie Dunn were sent to the Hartford Whalers for Mickey Volcan, a defenceman.

Even more exciting than the trades was the availability of previous draft choices. Right winger Hakan Loob, a ninth round draft in 1980, and a proven goal scorer in the Swedish Elite League, was reporting to training camp for the first time. Tim Hunter, the bruising winger who had played sixteen games the previous year, would be ready for his first full NHL season. And Al MacInnis, the Flames first round pick in the 1981 draft, was busy preparing himself, and his blistering shot from the point, for a full season on defence.

All in all, a lot of changes. It would be a Calgary Flames team with a whole new look. And why not? They would move to the newest building in the league. Last but not least, Coach Bob Johnson had filled a year's worth of notebooks, and with that first season

Eighteen-year-old centreman, and top draft pick, Dan Quinn scored almost a point a game in his first NHL season.

under his belt, the self-professed student of the game now had "the goods" on all of the other teams in the league.

Yes, the year had promise. Realistically, Coach Johnson and General Manager Fletcher didn't expect to catch the powerful Oilers immediately, but, promised Fletcher, "We'll be closer."

October 15, 1983. It was the season opener, and the new Olympic Saddledome was ready. A grand and gala opening was staged. The only problem that night was the opposition, as the Oilers edged the Flames in their home opener, 4-3. The team was then off for a five-game road trip, returning on October 25 to defeat the St. Louis Blues 5-4 and post their first two points in the Saddledome. They would go on to win 22 of their 40 home games, tying seven and losing only 11 games; a very respectable home record indeed. Unfortunately, their away record was 12 wins against 21 losses and seven ties.

Kent Nilsson again led the team in points over the regular season with 80, the third time in the four-year Calgary history that he had done so. But the surprise of the season was the performance of Eddie Beers who led

the Flames in scoring with 36 goals, and was second in overall points with 75. And young Dan Quinn finished with 52 points in only 53 games. Newly-acquired free agent defenceman Paul Baxter inherited the penalty minute title from Doug Risebrough in amassing 182 minutes.

The Flames finished with 82 points, four points more than the previous year, and two places higher in the overall standings at tenth. Their record was 34 wins, 32 losses and 14 ties. Once again, the Flames would face the third-place Canucks in the opening round of the Smythe Division playoffs.

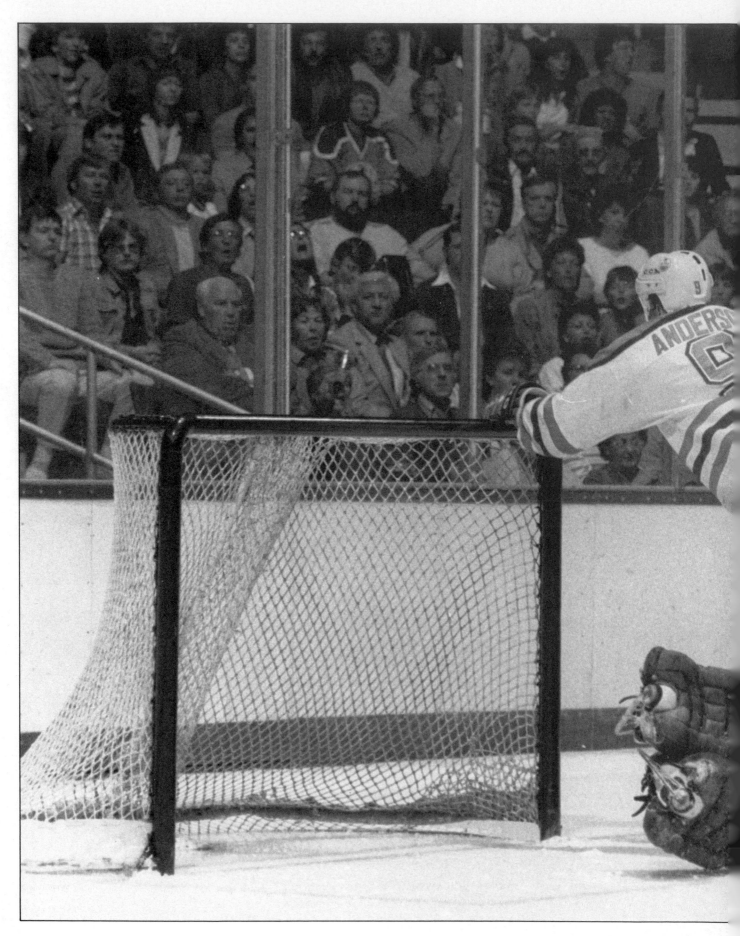

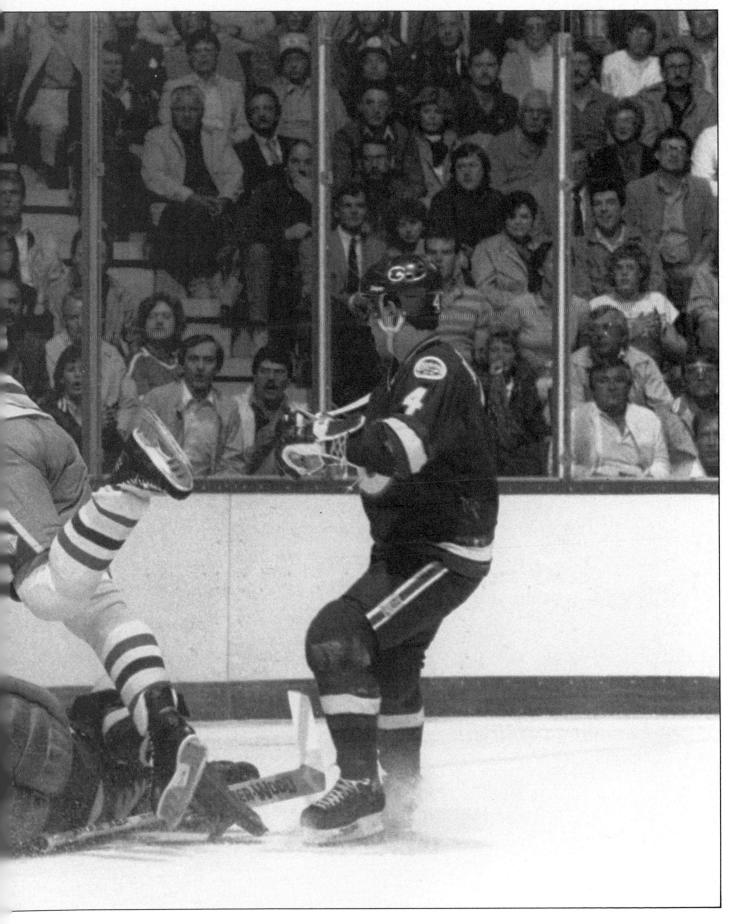

PLAYOFFS

March hadn't been kind to the Flames. Their dressing room looked like an emergency ward. Kent Nilsson had broken his ankle in a game against Los Angeles and was out for the season. Jamie Hislop had been accidentally clipped by a high stick in a game against the Islanders and was recovering from eye surgery and unable to play. Paul Reinhart, already suffering with a bad back, experienced a severe groin pull. Hakan Loob had twisted his ankle and wasn't 100 percent, while Mike Eaves had a bad knee. Colin Patterson and Jamie Macoun both were weakened with shoulder troubles and

LEFT:
Rugged defenceman Paul Baxter in his first year as a Flame. Baxter went on to play four seasons in Calgary. He retired in 1987 to become coach of Calgary's minor league affiliate, the Salt Lake City Golden Eagles.

RIGHT:
In the 1983-84 playoffs Paul Reinhart, pictured here with Lanny McDonald and Kari Eloranta, led the team in scoring with 17 points in 11 games.

Dave Hindmarch had suffered torn knee ligaments.

This arms-length list of walking wounded forced Coach Johnson's hand, and he had no choice but to play seven rookies — all with no previous NHL playoff experience. But experience wasn't a factor in the first two games at home as the Flames won the opener 5-3, and the second game 4-2. Was a sweep in the works? Not this time. Back on home ice the Canucks rebounded, shutting out the Flames 7-0. Johnson responded in game four at the Pacific Coliseum. He started Don Edwards in goal in place of Reggie Lemelin, and benched forwards Dan Quinn and Tim Hunter for Charlie Bourgeois and Steve Tambellini. And he surprised everybody when he moved Paul Reinhart from defence to centre. That proved to be crucial as Reinhart scored three goals, leading his team to a convincing 5-1 victory. It was the second straight year that the Flames had beaten the Canucks by the same first round playoff margin of three games to one.

Doug Risebrough.

The Oilers eliminated the Jets, and another round in the Battle of Alberta was set to begin.

One year earlier, the Flames lost to the Oilers. But Coach Bob Johnson and his scouting staff had now amassed two years worth of notebooks and video tapes on the Oilers. This was a much better Flames team.

The series opened in Edmonton. The Flames, who had a seven loss, one tie season record against the Oilers lost game one, 5-2. The next night, April 13, Calgary was a much different team. At the end of regulation play, the score was deadlocked, 5-5. Overtime wasn't long as Carey Wilson popped in the winner at 3:42 to even the series. It was the Flames' first playoff win in Edmonton.

The series moved to Calgary. But one thing this series didn't have, for either team, was home-ice advantage. The Oilers proved that by taking both games at the Saddledome, 3-2, and 5-3. It looked like it was all over for the Flames. But they refused to quit.

April 18 was the date, and the Oilers were looking to finish the series in front of their fans. Calgary foiled them by taking the fifth game with an exciting 5-4 win, and it was back to Calgary, where the fans were euphoric. A thousand came out to welcome their team at the airport. But that win, as big as it was, would be meaningless if they couldn't beat the Oilers in the Saddledome.

After three battle-scared periods the score was tied 4-4. In this series, in overtime, Calgary were unbeatable. And as he had so many other times over the years, Lanny McDonald was the hero with a goal after only 64 seconds. "That was all we asked for," said Coach Johnson afterwards. "One game, sudden death."

In game seven, the Flames lost three key players to injury early in the game — Paul Reinhart, Al MacInnis and Mike Eaves. Reinhart, who had completely controlled the blue line and played up to 40 minutes per game, had been the best player on the ice. His 17 playoffs points was tops for players not in the final. These injuries were a crushing blow to the Flames, and they lost the game (7-4), and the series.

Bob Johnson had asked for improvement, and he got it. "We're a lot better team coming out of this series than we were going in," he said. Wayne Gretzky, in the dressing room just down the hall, said "The Alberta rivalry is real."

As the team left the dressing room for the journey home, they became aware of something scribbled on the blackboard by the door. "I'm proud of you....Hold your heads high." Signed, Bob Johnson.

Teammates rush off the bench to congratulate Rejean Lemelin after the Flames defeated the Oilers 5-4 in game five of the Smythe Division final, played in Edmonton, April 18, 1984.

LEFT:
Lanny McDonald and Al MacInnis congratulate Carey Wilson after he scored the winning goal in overtime in game two of the Smythe Division final.

BELOW:
The rest of the team joins in the celebration.

1983-84 CALGARY FLAMES

TOP ROW: Steve Bozek, Steve Tambellini, Paul Reinhart, Carey Wilson, Colin Patterson, Kent Nilsson, Dan Quinn, Rich Kromm, Kari Eloranta.

THIRD ROW: Jim Murray (Trainer), Paul Baxter, Al MacInnis, Steve Konroyd, Eddy Beers, Charles Bourgeois, Jim Peplinski, Tim Hunter, Jamie Macoun, Bobby Stewart (Equipment Manager).

SECOND ROW: Al Murray (Assistant Trainer), Mike Eaves, Hakan Loob, Owners: Byron Seaman, Harley Hotchkiss, Norman Green, Daryl Seaman, Ralph Scurfield, Norman Kwong. Dave Hindmarch, Jim Jackson, Peter Marchuk.

FRONT ROW: Reggie Lemelin, Doug Risebrough (Co-captain), Bob Murdoch (Assistant Coach), Al Coates (Assistant to President), Cliff Fletcher (President and General Manager), Bob Johnson (Coach), Lanny McDonald (Co-captain), Don Edwards.

STATS

CALGARY FLAMES

REGULAR SEASON HIGHLIGHTS

Most Points
KENT NILSSON 80

Most Goals
EDDY BEERS 36

Most Assists
KENT NILSSON 49

Most Penalty Minutes
PAUL BAXTER 182

Most Wins Goalie
REJEAN LEMELIN 21

Trophies - Awards
NHL Rookie All-Star
HAKAN LOOB RW
JAMIE MACOUN DEF

Molson Cup
REJEAN LEMELIN

PLAYOFF HIGHLIGHTS

Most Points
PAUL REINHART 17

Most Goals
PAUL REINHART 6
LANNY McDONALD 6

Most Assists
AL MacINNIS 12

Most Penalty Minutes
PAUL BAXTER 37

Most Wins Goalie
REJEAN LEMELIN 4

Overtime Goals
CAREY WILSON 1
LANNY McDONALD 1

Don Edwards deflects the puck over the glass.

STATS

1983 - 84

Coach	REGULAR SEASON							PLAYOFFS				
	GP	W	L	T	PTS	GF	GA	GP	W	L	GF	GA
Bob Johnson	80	34	32	14	82	311	314	11	6	5	41	46

Mike Eaves vs. Ken Linseman.

Mike Vernon

The oddest note to this season was that Mike Vernon saw his first NHL action. Playing for only eleven minutes in one game, Vernon allowed four goals for a 21.82 goals per game average!

STATISTICS — REGULAR SEASON

PLAYER	GP	G	A	PTS	PIM
Kent Nilsson	67	31	49	80	22
Eddy Beers	73	36	39	75	88
Lanny McDonald	65	33	33	66	64
Hakan Loob	77	30	25	55	22
Dan Quinn	54	19	33	52	20
Doug Risebrough	77	23	28	51	161
Mike Eaves	61	14	36	50	20
Al MacInnis	51	11	34	45	42
Kari Eloranta	78	5	34	39	44
Jim Peplinski	74	11	22	33	114
Jamie Macoun	72	9	23	32	97
Colin Patterson	56	13	14	27	15
Paul Baxter	74	7	20	27	182
Steve Tambellini	73	15	10	25	16
Richard Kromm	53	11	12	23	27
Paul Reinhart	27	6	15	21	10
Steve Bozek	46	10	10	20	16
Jim Jackson	49	6	14	20	13
Steve Konroyd	80	1	13	14	94
Dave Hindmarch	29	6	5	11	2
Tony Stiles	30	2	7	9	20
Jamie Hislop	27	1	8	9	2
Tim Hunter	43	4	4	8	130
Carey Wilson	15	2	5	7	2
Mickey Volcan	19	1	4	5	18
Charles Bourgeois	17	1	3	4	35
Bruce Eakin	7	2	1	3	4
Kari Jalonen	9	0	3	3	0
Rejean Lemelin	51	0	3	3	6
Keith Hanson	25	0	2	2	77
Don Edwards	41	0	2	2	2
Neil Sheehy	1	1	0	1	2
Danny Bolduc	2	0	1	1	0
Mike Vernon	1	0	0	0	0
Jeff Brubaker	4	0	0	0	19
Totals	**80**	**311**	**512**	**823**	**1386**

GOALTENDERS	GP	MP	GA	AVG	W	L	T
Rejean Lemelin	51	2568	150	3.50	21	12	9
Don Edwards	41	2303	157	4.09	13	19	5
Mike Vernon	1	11	4	21.82	0	1	0
Totals		**4882**	**311**	**3.82**	**34**	**32**	**14**

ENG: Edwards (3)
SO: None

Tim Hunter and Dave Semenko. (Inset) Carey Wilson.

1984-85

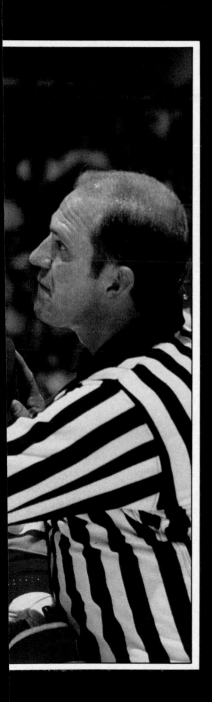

Calgary was definitely on a roll. They had taken the Oilers — who subsequently went on to win their first Stanley Cup — to a full seven games in last year's Smythe Division final. They had won two games on Edmonton ice. It was definitely something to build on.

In the June entry draft, Cliff Fletcher almost pulled off an incredible coup. Twice that spring Assistant General Manager Al MacNeil had flown to Europe for secret talks with a young Czechoslovakian defector. In April, a star eighteen-year-old defenceman had jumped from the National Team and was living in West Germany with his aunt. In Munich, the Flames signed Petr Svoboda to a letter of agreement should he be drafted by them in June. ''We thought we had everything under control,'' said Cliff Fletcher of the teenager who already played like a seasoned pro. But then the Quebec Nordiques found out, and subsequently the Montreal Canadiens, and Calgary — without a high first round draft pick — suddenly found themselves looking in from the outside. "We tried to trade up in the draft choices but we just couldn't make a deal," said Fletcher. At the draft, Montreal claimed Svoboda.

Nevertheless, Calgary had a great draft. Their first choice, 12th overall, was a feisty left winger from the Memorial Cup champion Ottawa 67s, Gary Roberts. Roberts was six foot two and 195 pounds, had an intimidating physical style, and played a position that Calgary had limited depth in. Only Eddy Beers and Richard Kromm were secure on the left side. Calgary's second and third choices were Ken Sabourin and Paul Ranheim. In the sixth round, Brett Hull was chosen, with Czechoslovakian Jiri Hrdina taken in the eight. And in the ninth round, a player was chosen who would have the greatest impact on the Flames of all their picks that year. Coach Johnson

Neil Sheehy

was extremely surprised that Gary Suter, a star University of Wisconsin defenceman, was still available.

Also during the off-season, a shuffle took place within Calgary's farm team. The Colorado Flames, along with Coach Pierre Page, would relocate to Moncton, New Brunswick. Page's Flames had become the class of the CHL, finishing in first place overall the previous year. The Calgary Flames were slowly becoming known NHL-wide as a team with depth.

As far as trades went, the off-season was quiet compared to previous years. In the spring, free agent Gino Cavallini was signed. Then, just as training camp started, Cliff

Fletcher signed big centre Joel Otto. The six foot four inch Otto would become a premier performer in the next few years.

The Flames got off to their best-ever start. After dropping the home opener to St. Louis 4-2, the Flames won seven of their next eight games. Over the entire season, Calgary registered 23 wins on home ice against only 11 losses and six ties, making Calgary one of the toughest stops around the league for visiting teams. On the road, the Flames improved their record 50 percent over the previous year, winning 18 games. Calgary finished the season with 95 points, their highest total ever. Goalie Reggie Lemelin played in 56 games, registering 30 wins against only 12 losses, and improving his goals against average to 3.46.

Kent Nilsson, again the team points leader, played in 77 games, scoring 37 goals and 62 assists for 99 points. Fellow countryman Hakan Loob had a strong season. His 37 goals tied Nilsson for the team lead, and his points total increased to 72 from 55 the previous season. Tim Hunter boomed to the top of the heap in penalty minutes with 259.

Overall, the Flames finished with their highest ranking ever — sixth place, a four place jump from the previous year.

However, another Smythe Division team improved even more. The Winnipeg Jets jumped from 73 points the previous year to 96 points, for fourth place in the league standings, and second place in the Smythe, one point ahead of Calgary. Los Angeles captured fourth spot, with the Canucks finishing out of the playoffs.

During the regular season, the Jets had been easy prey for the Flames, with Calgary winning five games, tying two, and losing only one. They had outscored the Jets by a margin of 49 to 31, with 15 power play goals. In one game in Calgary, on December 12, the Flames humiliated the Jets, 9-2.

Carey Wilson and Don Edwards combine to thwart an Oiler attacker.

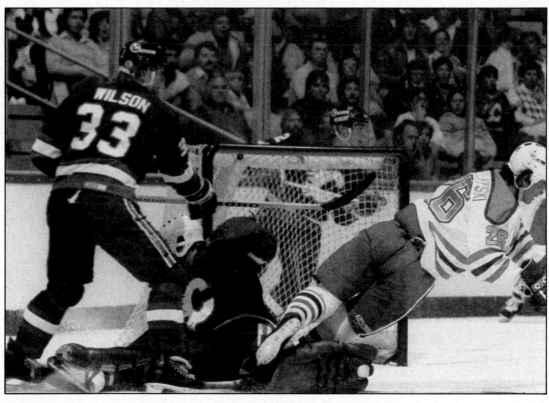

ABOVE:
Goaltender Don Edwards, acquired in a trade from Buffalo, played in 34 games during the 1984-85 season.

LEFT:
Steve Konroyd, who played in all 80 games during the 1983-84 season, was a solid, stay-at-home defenceman.

LEFT:
Perry Berezan came from college hockey to spark the Flames at centre.

Goaltender Don Edwards, plus Kent Nilsson (14) and Al MacInnis (2) combine to clear the puck. MacInnis, in his third season as a Flame, ranked sixth in team scoring with 14 goals and 52 assists. Nilsson led the team in scoring with 37 goals and 62 assists for 99 points.

CHARITY FUNDRAISING

Pictured below is the 1985 edition of the Flames Charity Slow Pitch Baseball Team. The team appears each year at a number of fundraising events in and around Calgary.

The Flames are also actively involved in an annual Celebrity Golf Tournament, which benefits Calgary Special Olympics; a Celebrity Dinner, with proceeds going to Aunts and Uncles at Large; an annual Hockey Clinic in aid of the Salvation Army Christmas Appeal Fund; and the Calgary Firefighters Toys For Tots campaign. The wives of the players also sponsor their own Charity Fundraiser.

TOP ROW: *(left to right)* Peter Maher, Dan Quinn, Al MacInnis, Jamie Macoun, Colin Patterson, Doug Risebrough, Al Coates, Cliff Fletcher, Stu Hendry.
BOTTOM: Honorary Flame, Paul Baxter, Jim Peplinski, Lanny McDonald, Steve Konroyd, Mike Vernon, Rick Skaggs.
FRONT: Trevor Taylor, Mary Jane Kletke.

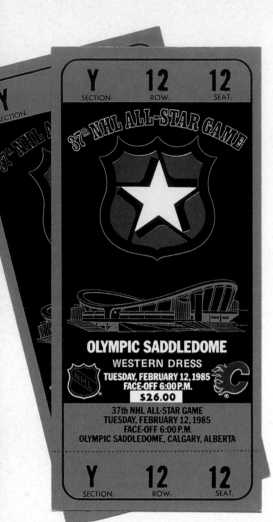

CALGARY HOSTS THE 1985 ALL-STAR GAME

February 12, 1985 was a proud day for both the City of Calgary and the Calgary Flames hockey club as the 37th Annual All-Star Game and Gala was held in Calgary. Paul Reinhart and Al MacInnis were chosen to represent the Flames. The festivities and the game were a total success, and were completely sold out. More than $100,000 was raised for charity.

Glenn Hall, the Calgary Flames goaltending coach, was named the honourary Captain of the Campbell Conference team, while Guy Lafleur was honorary Captain of the Wales team. The Wales team won 6-4, with Mario Lemieux named as the game's MVP.

Al MacInnis

Paul Reinhart

Glenn Hall

1984 - 85 CALGARY FLAMES

FOURTH ROW — L to R: Paul Baxter, Steve Bozek, Yves Courteau, Kari Eloranta, Dave Hindmarch, Steve Tambellini, Richard Kromm, Dan Quinn, Kent Nilsson.

THIRD ROW: Peter Marchuk (Fitness Consultant), Colin Patterson, Carey Wilson, Tim Hunter, Eddy Beers, Charles Bourgeois, Jim Peplinski, (Co-captain), Jamie Macoun, Al MacInnis, Steve Konroyd, Jim Murray (Trainer).

SECOND ROW: Jamie Hislop (Assistant Coach), Paul Reinhart, Mike Eaves, Owners: Norman Kwong, Ralph Scurfield, Norman Green, Harley Hotchkiss, Daryl Seaman, Byron Seaman. Jim Jackson, Hakan Loob, Bobby Stewart (Equipment Manager), Al Murray (Assistant Trainer).

FRONT ROW: Rejean Lemelin, Lanny McDonald (Co-captain), Bob Murdoch (Assistant Coach), Al Coates (Assistant to President), Cliff Fletcher (President & General Manager), Al MacNeil (Assistant General Manager), Bob Johnson (Coach), Doug Risebrough (Co-captain), Don Edwards.

MISSING: Joel Otto, Gino Cavallini, Perry Berezan.

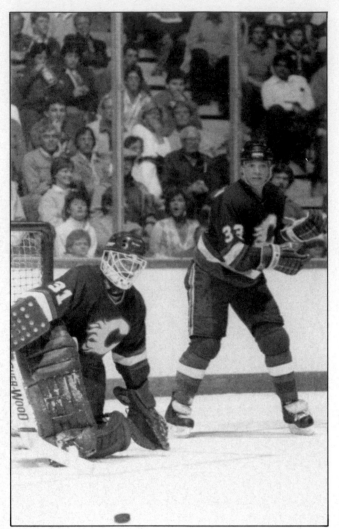

PLAYOFFS

The Smythe Division semi-final opened in Winnipeg. Reggie Lemelin, who had been in nets for all five Flames league victories over the Jets, got the call. In the series opener, the game ended regulation time deadlocked 4-4. But the Flames overtime playoff magic of the previous year was not to be, and the Jets scored at 7:56 of overtime. In the second game, the Flames lost, 5-2. Back to the Saddledome, the Flames did not disappoint, jumping out to an early lead, and a 4-0 shutout win. But it was all over in game four, as Winnipeg beat the Flames 5-3, winning the series.

ABOVE:
Reggie Lemelin and Carey Wilson.

RIGHT:
Two of the league's most tenacious centremen — Doug Risebrough and Laurie Boschman — face off.

STATS

1984-85

Coach	REGULAR SEASON							PLAYOFFS				
	GP	W	L	T	PTS	GF	GA	GP	W	L	GF	GA
Bob Johnson	80	46	31	3	95	318	289	6	2	4	15	22

REGULAR SEASON HIGHLIGHTS

Most Points
KENT NILSSON 99

Most Goals
KENT NILSSON 37
HAKAN LOOB 37

Most Assists
KENT NILSSON 62

Most Penalty Minutes
TIM HUNTER 259

Most Wins Goalie
REJEAN LEMELIN 30

Molson Cup
REJEAN LEMELIN

PLAYOFF HIGHLIGHTS

Most Points
HAKAN LOOB 6

Most Goals
HAKAN LOOB 3

Most Assists
STEVE KONROYD 4

Most Penalty Minutes
TIM HUNTER 24

Most Wins Goalie
REJEAN LEMELIN 1

STATISTICS — REGULAR SEASON

PLAYER	GP	G	A	PTS	PIM
Kent Nilsson	77	37	62	99	14
Hakan Loob	78	37	35	72	14
Carey Wilson	74	24	48	72	27
Paul Reinhart	75	23	46	69	18
Eddy Beers	74	28	40	68	94
Al MacInnis	67	14	52	66	75
Dan Quinn	74	20	38	58	22
Richard Kromm	73	20	32	52	32
Jim Peplinski	80	16	29	45	111
Colin Patterson	57	22	21	43	5
Mike Eaves	56	14	29	43	10
Jamie Macoun	70	9	30	39	67
Lanny McDonald	43	19	18	37	36
Steve Bozek	54	13	22	35	6
Steve Tambellini	47	19	10	29	4
Steve Konroyd	64	3	23	26	73
Tim Hunter	71	11	11	22	259
Paul Baxter	70	5	14	19	126
Gino Cavallini	27	6	10	16	14
Kari Eloranta	65	2	11	13	39
Doug Risebrough	15	7	5	12	49
Joel Otto	17	4	8	12	30
Charles Bourgeois	47	2	10	12	134
Neil Sheehy	31	3	4	7	109
Perry Berezan	9	3	2	5	4
Jim Jackson	10	1	4	5	0
Yves Courteau	14	1	4	5	4
Bruce Eakin	1	0	0	0	0
Don Edwards	34	0	0	0	4
Rejean Lemelin	56	0	0	0	4
Totals	**80**	**363**	**618**	**981**	**1384**

GOALTENDERS	GP	MP	GA	AVG	W	L	T
Rejean Lemelin	56	3176	183	3.46	30	12	10
Don Edwards	34	1691	115	4.08	11	15	2
Totals		**4867**	**298**	**3.67**	**41**	**27**	**12**

ENG: Lemelin (3), Edwards
SO: Lemelin, Edwards

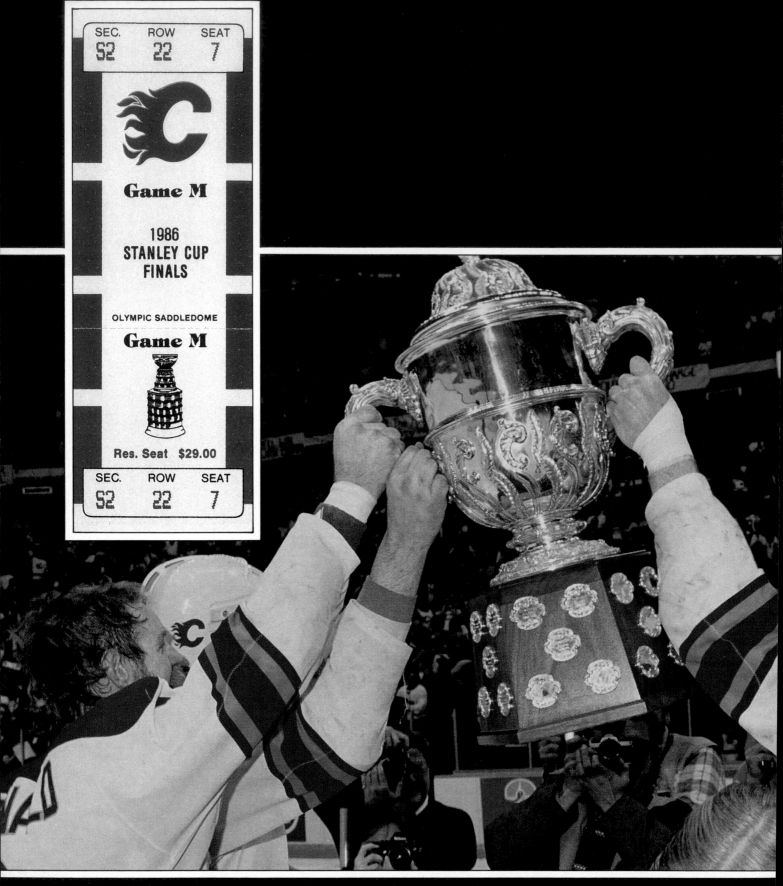

SEC. 52 ROW 22 SEAT 7

C

Game M

1986
STANLEY CUP
FINALS

OLYMPIC SADDLEDOME

Game M

Res. Seat $29.00

SEC. 52 ROW 22 SEAT 7

Co-captains McDonald, Peplinski and Risebrough raise the Campbell Conference Bowl.

1985-86

Kent Nilsson, Calgary's all-time leading scorer, was gone. In a June trade that many fans viewed with mixed emotions, Cliff Fletcher sent Nilsson (plus a draft pick) to the Minnesota North Stars in exchange for two second round draft picks. The high-scoring Swedish right winger had led the team in scoring four of the five seasons the Flames had been in Calgary. But it was his playoff performances, particularly in the previous year's loss to the Jets, that had disappointed the Flames management. Playing in three of the four games against Winnipeg, he registered only one point, an assist. In a total of 29 playoff games, Nilsson had four goals and 24 assists for 28 points, while in 345 regular season games he had scored 189 goals and 280 assists for 469 points. The five-year love-hate relationship with Kent Nilsson was now over.

The first of the second round picks that Calgary received from the North Stars turned out to be their future Rookie-of-the-Year, Joe Nieuwendyk. Their second pick, exercised in 1987, was Stephane Matteau, a left winger from the Hull Juniors.

A quiet summer followed in the trade circuit. With the exception of Nilsson, the Flames roster would be virtually the same one that lost to Winnipeg last April. Joe Nieuwendyk wasn't expected to make the team in his first year so, in effect, the team would begin the season with 99 fewer points in the line-up. Others on the roster would have to pick up that slack.

One new face in the line-up was 24-year-old goaltender Marc D'Amour. He had spent three years in the Flames system, the first two in Colorado and the previous season split between Moncton and Salt Lake. After battling with another Flames hopeful, Mike Vernon, D'Amour had emerged as the number one goaltender in Moncton. This season he would get his chance to back-up Calgary's starting goalie, Reggie Lemelin.

Joe Mullen

The Flames started tentatively. After five games, their record stood at two wins and three losses. But it got better, and after ten games they were .500. Then the team took off. By December 10, they had 33 points and a 15-win, 8-loss, 3-tie record, good enough for third place overall in the league.

December 14, 1985, wasn't expected to be a date included in any Flames historical guide, but on that date the Flames lost to the Canucks 4-3. It would be almost a full month — and ten frustrating losses — before they won another game. "All of a sudden, the things that were bouncing for us are now bouncing against us," said Coach Bob

Johnson. "I've seen some bad streaks before, believe me," said Co-captain Doug Risebrough. "But never anything like this. Now we're frustrated."

The Flames partly relieved their frustration against a touring Russian team, Moscow Dynamo, on December 29 at the Saddledome. An exuberant crowd watched Calgary beat the Russians 3-2 for the Soviets only loss of their NHL tour. Mike Vernon, who started the game because of a slight injury to Marc D'Amour, picked up his first win as a Calgary Flame. But unfortunately for Vernon, the victory didn't count in the NHL standings.

The Flames ended the first half of their season (40 games) with a victory against the Canucks, the team responsible for starting Calgary's ten-game losing streak. That win was significant in two ways: firstly, it ushered in the second half of the season; and secondly, it was the first regular season game start for young rookie goaltender Mike Vernon. Over the last 40 games the Flames caught fire, winning 22, losing only 12, and tying 5, good for sixth place overall for the second straight season. More importantly, it gave them second place in the Smythe Division and home-ice advantage in the first round of the playoffs.

About mid-February, Mike Vernon — the Calgary native and former member of the Calgary Wranglers — assumed the majority of the goaltending duties from Lemelin. Vernon compiled an end of season record of nine wins, three losses and three ties, with four of those wins coming in his last four games. But no win that entire season would loom larger than the 9-3 blasting the Flames gave the Oilers on their last regular season meeting, April 4, 1986. Until that

Marc D'Amour

game they'd managed only one point against Edmonton in their previous seven games. It turned out to be the turning point in the Flames — Oilers rivalry. In that Friday night contest, 242 penalty minutes were logged. Edmonton Coach Glen Sather was kicked out of the game. Twelve goals had been scored, and nine of them were for Calgary. The Oilers had been humbled. For the fans, there was immense gratification. For the Calgary players, there was a new feeling of confidence.

Winnipeg had finished third in the Smythe with 59 points, 30 fewer than Calgary. In their regular season matchups, the Flames came out on top with six wins, one tie, and one loss, and they had beaten the Jets the last five games straight. It looked like this might be the year for the Flames to exact revenge against the teams that had previously eliminated them from the playoffs. And there were some major additions that would definitely help the club in their playoff drive.

For starters, there was the big trade made on February 1. Popular defenceman Charlie Bourgeois, and left wingers Eddy Beers and Gino Cavallini had been sent to St. Louis in exchange for Joe Mullen, Terry Johnson, and Rik Wilson. With the acquisition of Mullen, Coach Johnson now had a game-breaker. Mullen played 29 games for the Flames and, along with the totals from his 48 games with the Blues, would lead Calgary in scoring with 44 goals and 46 assists for 90 points. At this same time, Hakan Loob started to come on strong, and newcomer Vernon was solid in goal.

Another late-season trade brought New York Islanders veteran winger and clutch playoff scorer John Tonelli to Calgary, in exchange for Richard Kromm and Steve Konroyd. Also acquired in a late season transaction was tough guy Nick Fotiu. All of the pieces necessary for playoff success seemed to be in place.

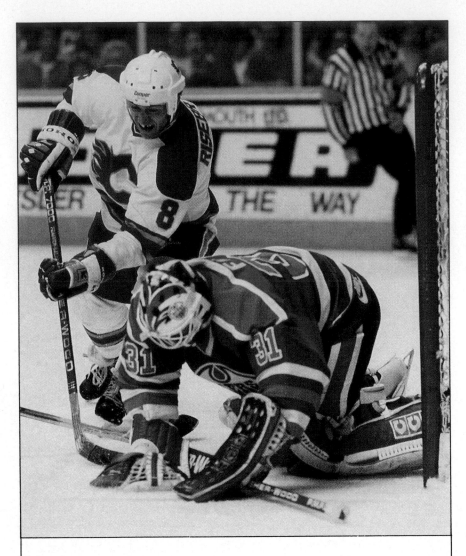

Doug Risebrough

"It was the turning point of the season — a 9-3 drubbing of the Oilers in our final game of the regular season."

Coach Bob Johnson

OPPOSITE PAGE:
Newcomers Nick Fotiu (inset) and John Tonelli added experience and muscle to the club.

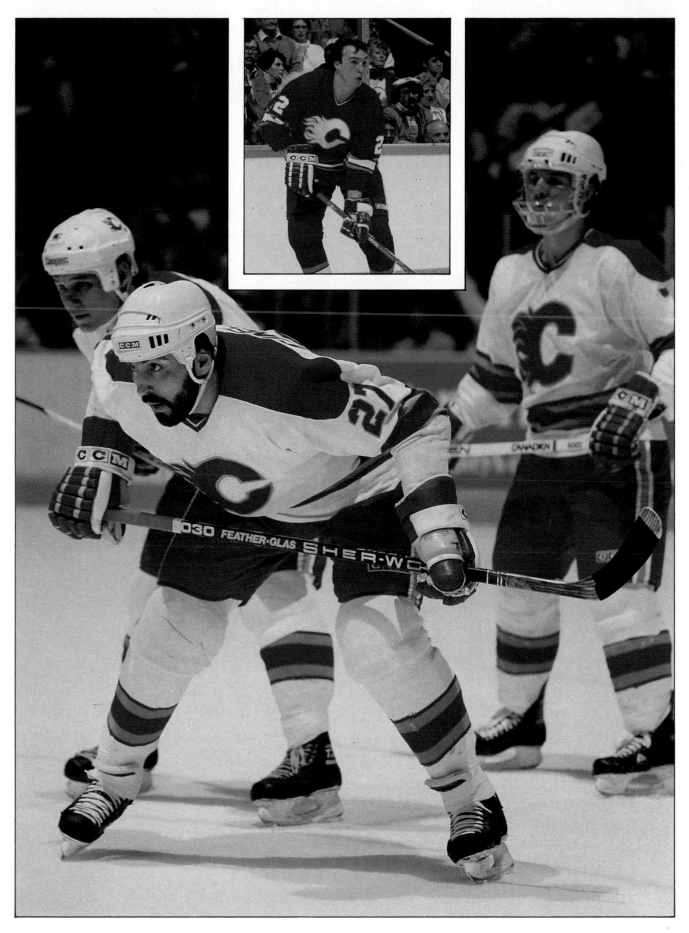

PLAYOFFS
CALGARY vs. WINNIPEG

Three games after the Winnipeg-Calgary series started, it was over. The team that had so unceremoniously dumped the Flames the previous year in the playoffs was now gone. Calgary dominated the first two games at home, 5-1 and 6-4. The third game, in Winnipeg, saw Lanny McDonald ice the series victory with an overtime goal. In the other Smythe Division matchup, the first place Oilers dispatched Vancouver, 3-0, and it was on to the series that everyone was waiting for.

PLAYOFFS
CALGARY vs. EDMONTON

"We knew we had to be sharp against the Canucks if we were going to be ready for Calgary in the next round," said Wayne Gretzky after the Oilers had knocked out the Canucks in three straight games. "After all, Calgary is going to be ready for us." That turned out to be the understatement of the year.

Talk of an impending war abounded. Marty McSorley of the Oilers offered, "The Canucks were the sparring partner before the real fight." Doug Risebrough responded, "We're going into this for one reason, and that's to win, at whatever cost." In their last regular season meeting, 242 penalty minutes had been called.

"You develop a lot of character through adversity, and certainly we've had lots of adversity playing against the Oilers," said defenceman Paul Baxter.

Coach Johnson often used golf-related analogies. "Beating Edmonton," he said, "is even more difficult to imagine for us because they have dominated us for such a long time. It's like when you broke par on a golf course, shot 69; you know it can be done because you've done it. One big plus for us was that 9-3 victory we had over them on the last weekend of the season. We finally beat them, shot our 69."

The Flames travelled to Edmonton to open the series at the Coliseum on April 18. A shocker. Calgary defeated Edmonton 4-1 in the first game. "We're one under par," declared Johnson. In the second game, Glenn Anderson scored at 1:04 of overtime to tie the series at one. Game three, back at the Saddledome, it was a 3-2 victory for the Flames. Coach Johnson said they were now two under par. Game four was 7-4 for the Oilers.

MacInnis, Macoun and Peplinski.

This game marked goalie Mike Vernon's first loss of the playoffs, and his first loss overall since February 23. His record was 12-0-1, including 5-0 in the playoffs.

Again the series was tied. Calgary won game five, again on away ice, by a 4-1 margin. "Our guys had great concentration tonight," said Coach Johnson. "We had a lot of overachievers out there. We've got guys playing above and beyond their talents, and that's what it's all about in playoff hockey." Joe Mullen had one assist in the game five victory over the Oilers, extending his playoff scoring streak to eight consecutive games, with six goals and four assists.

For some reason, home ice again had no bearing in this series. With a game six win by the Oilers in Calgary, each team had won two games in the other's building. This was a good sign for the Flames, because the seventh and deciding game would be played in Edmonton. Calgary jumped out to a 2-0 early lead but the Oilers clawed their way back with two goals to tie the game 2-2. Then, at 5:14 of the third period, Oiler defenceman Steve Smith, on his birthday, made the blunder of a lifetime by banking a clearing pass off his goalie, Grant Fuhr, that bounced into the net. Perry Berezan, an Edmonton native, had been the last Flame to touch the puck, and even though he was sitting on the bench when the puck went into the net, he was credited with the biggest goal, up to then, in Flames history. Bedlam ensued.

Bob Johnson credited his team's three game sweep over the Jets. This had given the Flames four days to focus on Edmonton. And his game plan was executed to perfection.

Before the series, Paul Reinhart had stated: "Everything we do from September to April is compared to and plotted against how Edmonton did. They're the ones to catch. If you win 72 games a year and lose the eight against Edmonton, where are you? Nowhere. We can try to fool ourselves and say we are trying to be as good as the Washington Capitals, but that's not what we're trying to do. We're trying to catch Edmonton."

Well, in a seven-game series, played between two teams with the hottest rivalry in the NHL, Reinhart's words would be prophetic.

They had caught and buried the Oilers. Twenty thousand fans poured into and outside Calgary's International Airport to greet their heroes on their return later that night. A two-mile long traffic jam developed outside the airport and a crowd thirty deep lined the fence by the runway. It was rush hour downtown, and it was 1:00 in the morning. A city truly celebrated. The Calgary Flames were the Smythe Division Champions.

BELOW:
Neil Sheehy (5) and Gary Suter (20). Suter and Carey Wilson (bottom) were both lost to the Flames for the duration of the playoffs due to injuries sustained in the Flames - Oilers series.

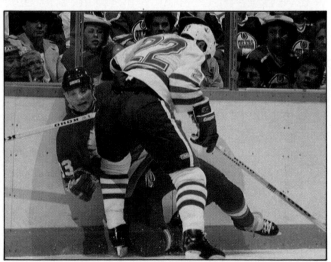

BELOW:
Paul Reinhart terminates Messier's forward progress.

ABOVE RIGHT:
Mike Vernon and Steve Bozek savour the victory!

ABOVE LEFT:
Celebration reigns after eliminating the Oilers!

LEFT:
(L to R) Gerry Blair, Al Coates and Cliff Fletcher.

BELOW LEFT:
Lanny McDonald.

BELOW RIGHT:
Perry Berezan got credit for the game-winning goal.

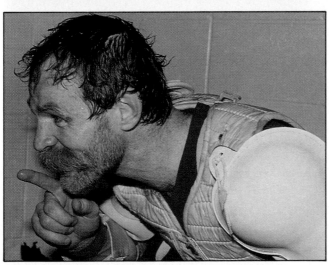

ABOVE:

In the dressing room, Colin Patterson (left) and Steve Bozek celebrate their victory.

LEFT:

Stepping off the airplane, Gary Suter (left) and Hakan Loob greet the thousands of fans who came to meet them at the airport.

LEFT:

Al Murray, Assistant Trainer, is escorted by a policeman back to the Flames' bench.

"One of the Oilers hit Gary Suter into the boards just down from our bench, and his stick flew up into the crowd. In the heat of the moment I jumped into the stands to get it back. I got about half way to it when I started to get booed but I couldn't turn back then. I grabbed the stick but one of the fans wouldn't let go. Push led to shove and the next thing I knew was Dad (Trainer Bearcat Murray) had jumped over the boards to help. It was one of those spur of the moment things, and it was the stick Suter had used all series. When I gave it back to him, the next shift he scored a goal with it. When Bearcat jumped over the boards to help me, he pulled the tendons in his leg and ended up having to use crutches." — Al Murray.

COACH JOHNSON'S SEVEN POINT PLAN

"During the 1985 - 86 regular season, we knew that we couldn't just go into the play-offs and say we were going to play the Oilers head to head. We knew they were a better team than we were. We had to devise a plan that our players could believe in. We devised the Seven Point Plan and put it into effect for the last two games of the season. In the first game we tied the Oilers 4-4, and then in the final game of the regular season we scored five power play goals and beat them 9-3. That gave our team confidence that the plan would work in the playoffs."

The Seven Point Plan was:

1) We wanted to leave their tough guys on the ice. McSorley, McClelland and Semenko. We didn't want to get involved with their tough guys. We wanted to keep them on the ice because if they were playing, then we didn't have to be concerned with stopping Gretzky, Messier and Kurri.

2) We had to key on Gretzky. When Gretzky was on the ice, we wanted Neil Sheehy on defence against him and either Carey Wilson or Doug Risebrough at centre. Sheehy was able to get under Gretzky's skin, constantly yapping at him and hitting him behind the net and just generally bothering him. In one game Neil came to me on the bench and said that Gretzky had called him a goon and said that he shouldn't even be on the ice. I told Sheehy to go back out there and look Gretzky straight in the eye and tell him,

"All I'm trying to do is get enough money to buy a new car. You've got about eleven new ones." Sheehy was a role player and he accepted the challenge. He had the Oilers worrying more about Sheehy and less about the game.

3) Paul Coffey was one of their key players. In order to neutralize him, we felt that our right winger would have to go at Coffey. When he would give and go, we would try to bump him. Then when he went up the ice and into our end, we tried to get in front of him, interfere with him, and hold him up from getting back into the play quickly. This meant that when we counter-attacked, we would be facing only one defenceman instead of two.

4) We had to close the gap between our forwards and our defencemen. It took away their criss-crossing patterns, and then on the counter-attack, move the puck straight ahead to the man in front and none of those cross-ice passes. We ended up with more three on twos than they did. It was very effective.

5) We knew that Messier, Anderson and Gretzky always went up the left side, so we keyed on that area, not giving them the blueline on the left side. This forced them to make a play on the other side of the blueline.

6) Colin Patterson's job was to delay and generally demoralize Jari Kurri, to stop him from getting the clear passes from Gretzky.

7) We had to get ahead of Edmonton early, to shut down their offense.

PLAYOFFS
CALGARY vs. ST. LOUIS

There was another hurdle to overcome, however, before sights could be set on the Stanley Cup. The St. Louis Blues. And Calgary had lost five of their last six regular season games against the Blues. The Flames had needed the full seven games to defeat the Oilers, so Coach Johnson wouldn't have the luxury of a three or four day practice session. The players had come through a grueling series, both physically and emotionally, but a rest was simply not possible. Injured players would have to play with their injuries.

The Flames opened against the Blues on home ice May 2.

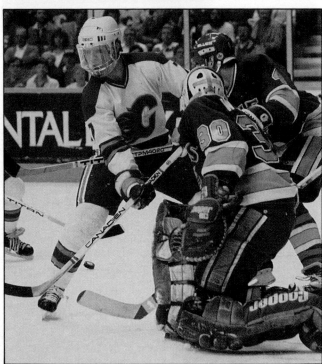

They were tired, listless, and the Blues won, 3-2. Game two was an entirely different story. After their wake-up call in game one, Doug Risebrough rose to the occasion, scoring his first ever playoff hat trick. Calgary won 8-2. In game three, in St. Louis, Calgary scored after only twenty seconds and went on to win 5-3. But St. Louis came roaring back in game four to tie the series with a 5-2 victory.

Back in Calgary, the Flames won game five 4-2, and quickly left for St. Louis hoping to wrap up the series. But it wasn't to be. Leading 5-2 with only twelve minutes left in the third, the Flames were shocked when Paslawski scored, then Sutter, then Paslawski again. Suddenly the game was tied, and going into overtime. Joe Mullen's slapshot had the Blues' goalie beaten, but it hit the crossbar. A few minutes later, Wickenheiser scored, and the series was tied at three. Home for the final game, the Flames forechecked the Blues into oblivion, allowing only 18 shots on goal, and winning 2-1 on goals by MacInnis and Patterson. A second banner was soon to be raised — Campbell Conference Champions!

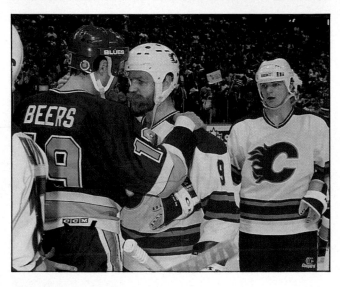

TOP:

The C of Red.

MIDDLE:

Joe Mullen — a former St. Louis Blue — almost scores on Rick Wamsley — a future Calgary Flame.

LEFT:

Eddy Beers congratulates ex-teammate Lanny McDonald after the win, as Al MacInnis looks on.

THE STANLEY CUP FINAL
CALGARY vs. MONTREAL

Calgary finished higher overall than the Canadiens and had home-ice advantage for the final round. The Flames started off the series by showing the same grit and determination that had gotten them past the Oilers. They dominated the Canadiens in every category and, with the fans behind the goal putting the Roo-Waah hex on netminder Patrick Roy, the Flames startled Montreal with an opening 5-2 victory.

Montreal's Coach Jean Perron used the day off between games to plan his strategy. He planned to attack while killing penalties, and keep a Montreal forward right at the Calgary

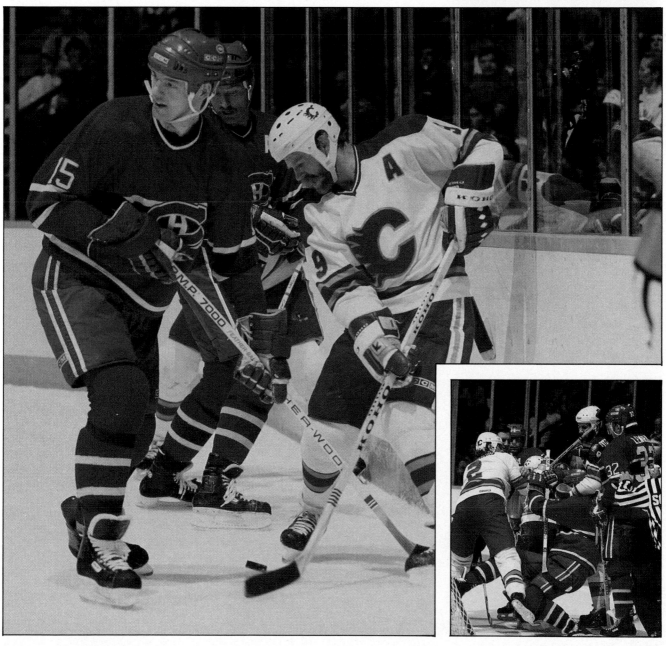

blueline whenever the puck was in the centre ice zone, forcing the Calgary defencemen back. This, in turn, would open up the centre ice area for his skaters. It proved effective and, with the addition of running the Calgary goalie whenever possible, it helped turn the series around. In game two, Brian Skrudland scored the winning goal in overtime, Patrick Roy had shed the hex, and the Canadiens had won 3-2, evening the series at one game apiece. The Flames were hit with injuries. Missing from the line-up were Gary Suter, Carey Wilson, Colin Patterson and Nick Fotiu. All were sorely missed in game three at the Montreal Forum. After a quick 2-1 Calgary lead, the wheels fell off. Three Montreal goals in 68 seconds and the game was basically over. And Joe Mullen, the Flames' top scorer, was sidelined for at least a game with a neck injury after being checked head first into the boards. The Flames missed his scoring prowess in game four, losing 1-0 in a tight defensive game.

It was back to the Saddledome for game five, with the Flames down 3-1 in the series. Early in the third period, the Canadiens had taken a 4-1 lead. Then, with less than four minutes left in the game, Steve Bozek scored his second of the night to bring the Flames within two. Calgary pulled their goalie and, with 46 seconds left, Joe Mullen, wearing a neck brace, scored again. The Flames had come back to within one goal. In the final few seconds Calgary stormed the net, forcing Roy to make several desperate saves. But time ran out, and Roy preserved the win, and the victory, for the Canadiens. Calgary fans got half the cake they had wanted. They had seen the Stanley Cup presented at centre ice, but they would have to wait before the Cup could stay in Calgary.

Calgary had made some giant strides, however. Making it past the Oilers for the first time. Smythe Division Champions for the first time. Campbell Conference Champions for the first time. Stanley Cup finalists for the first time. Yes, the fans were satisfied. Their team had come through for them.

In the awards category, the Flames had been recognized. Gary Suter won the Calder Trophy for Rookie-of-the-Year, and he was named to the NHL Rookie All-Star team. Hakan Loob won his first Molson Cup. Joe Mullen had taken over as Calgary's offensive star. Mike Vernon demonstrated he could become the best goaltender in the NHL. And Al MacInnis had shown his potential to control the blueline, especially on the power play. Yes, it had been a good season, and the many thousands of fans who attended the subsequent parade, plus a sold-out crowd at the Saddledome in the final minutes of the final game, showed their support by chanting *"Thank You Flames, Thank You Flames!"*

Doug Risebrough and Larry Robinson.

Larry Robinson, quoted after the '86 Stanley Cup finals:

"We outlasted the Flames, but it was a lot closer than any one of us would want to admit. When the Flames started their comeback in the third period of the final game, our team panicked. Our bench was in turmoil."

1985- 86 CALGARY FLAMES

FOURTH ROW: (left to right) Nick Fotiu, Al MacInnis, Tim Hunter, Terry Johnson, Jamie Macoun, Neil Sheehy, Joel Otto, Carey Wilson.

THIRD ROW: Al Murray (Assistant Trainer), Jim Peplinski (Co-Captain), Owners: Byron Seaman, Daryl Seaman, Harley Hotchkiss, Norman Green, Norman Kwong, Sonia Scurfield. Paul Reinhart, Bobby Stewart (Equipment Manager).

SECOND ROW: Perry Berezan, Paul Baxter, Steve Bozek, Hakan Loob, Joe Mullen, Dan Quinn, Gary Suter, Colin Patterson, John Tonelli, Jim Murray (Head Trainer).

FRONT ROW: Rejean Lemelin, Doug Risebrough (Co-Captain), Pierre Page (Assistant Coach), Bob Murdoch (Assistant Coach), Bob Johnson (Head Coach), Cliff Fletcher (President and General Manager), Al MacNeil (Assistant General Manager), Al Coates (Assistant to President), Lanny McDonald (Co-Captain), Mike Vernon.

STATS

CALGARY FLAMES

REGULAR SEASON HIGHLIGHTS

Most Points
JOE MULLEN 90
(Calgary 38, St. Louis 52)

Most Goals
JOE MULLEN 44
(Calgary 16, St. Louis 28)

Most Assists
AL MacINNIS 57

Most Penalty Minutes
TIM HUNTER 291

Most Wins Goalie
REJEAN LEMELIN 29

Trophies - Awards
Calder Trophy
NHL Rookie All-Star Defence
GARY SUTER

Molson Cup
HAKAN LOOB

PLAYOFF HIGHLIGHTS

Most Points
AL MacINNIS 19
JOE MULLEN 19

Most Goals
JOE MULLEN 12

Most Assists
AL MacINNIS 15

Most Penalty Minutes
TIM HUNTER 108

Most Wins Goalie
MIKE VERNON 12

Overtime Goals
LANNY McDONALD 1

Gary Suter, who was drafted in the 9th round, 180th overall in the 1984 entry draft, had a fantastic rookie season. He won the Calder Trophy as Rookie-of-the-Year, the first Calgary Flame to do so, and third in the history of the franchise. In the process, Suter set five team records and was chosen to the All-Star team. He played in all 80 games, scoring 18 goals and adding 50 assists, the second highest all-time points scored (68) by a defenceman in his rookie season.

STATS

1985-86

Coach	REGULAR SEASON							PLAYOFFS				
	GP	W	L	T	PTS	GF	GA	GP	W	L	GF	GA
Bob Johnson	80	40	31	9	89	354	315	22	12	10	81	69

Bob Johnson on the Montreal Series

"If we had had three or four days to prepare against Montreal, I am convinced we would have won it. It was our own fault, going seven games with Edmonton and then another seven games with St. Louis. Seeing those thousands of fans at the airport when we came back from Edmonton, all the emotion, and then having to go right into the series with St. Louis. When we lost that first game against the Blues 3-2 in the last few minutes of the game, I couldn't believe it. Then we lost the sixth game which we should have won. We were up 5-2, and they didn't have a shot for fourteen minutes. It was just one of those things that happens in hockey. You can't explain it. I've watched that tape so many times. If we had won that sixth game, we would have won the Cup.

In the finals they beat us in overtime in the second game, and then 1-0 in Montreal, and then 4-3 in the final game. That series was a lot closer than one might think."

Hakan Loob

STATISTICS — REGULAR SEASON

PLAYER		GP	G	A	PTS	PIM
Joe Mullen	ST.L.	48	28	24	52	10
	Cal.	29	16	22	38	11
	Tot.	77	44	46	90	21
Dan Quinn		78	30	42	72	44
Lanny McDonald		80	28	43	71	44
John Tonelli	NYI	65	20	41	61	50
	Cal.	9	3	4	7	10
	Tot.	74	23	45	68	60
Gary Suter		80	18	50	68	141
Al MacInnis		77	11	57	68	76
Hakan Loob		68	31	36	67	36
Joel Otto		79	25	34	59	188
Jim Peplinski		77	24	35	59	214
Carey Wilson		76	29	29	58	24
Steve Bozek		64	21	22	43	24
Doug Risebrough		62	15	28	43	169
Perry Berezan		55	12	21	33	39
Paul Reinhart		32	8	25	33	15
Jamie Macoun		77	11	21	32	81
Richard Kromm		63	12	17	29	31
Colin Patterson		61	14	13	27	22
Steve Konroyd		59	7	20	27	64
Eddy Beers		33	11	10	21	8
Neil Sheehy		65	2	16	18	271
Tim Hunter		66	8	7	15	291
Gino Cavallini		27	7	7	14	26
Charles Bourgeois		29	5	5	10	128
Terry Johnson	ST.L.	49	0	4	4	87
	Cal.	24	1	4	5	71
	Tot.	73	1	8	9	158
Paul Baxter		47	4	3	7	194
Rejean Lemelin		60	0	5	5	10
Rik Wilson	ST.L.	32	0	4	4	48
	Cal.	2	0	0	0	0
	Tot.	34	0	4	4	48
Yves Courteau		4	1	1	2	0
Brian Bradley		5	0	1	1	0
Nick Fotiu		9	0	1	1	21
Mike Vernon		18	0	1	1	4
Robin Bartel		1	0	0	0	0
Dale Degray		1	0	0	0	0
Mark Lamb		1	0	0	0	0
Marc D'Amour		16	0	0	0	22
Totals		80	354	580	934	2279

GOALTENDERS	GP	MP	GA	AVG	W	L	T
Mike Vernon	18	921	52	3.39	9	3	3
Marc D'Amour	15	560	32	3.43	2	4	2
Rejean Lemelin	60	3369	229	4.08	29	24	4
Totals		4850	313	3.87	40	31	9

ENG: Lemelin (2)
SO: Vernon, Lemelin

Colin Patterson. (Inset) Mike Bullard.

1986-87

As always, the new season started with the June entry draft. In their second pick, 37th overall, the Flames selected big defenceman Brian Glynn from the Saskatoon Blades. With their first pick they chose George Pelawa, an 18-year-old right winger from Bimidji High School in Minnesota. At six foot three inches tall, he would possibly be an impact player within a couple of years. But in August came the tragic news — Pelawa had been killed in an automobile accident. It was a tremendous shock to the Flames organization and set the tone for a quiet training camp some ten days later.

Overall, however, the prospects looked good. Joe Mullen had been 14th in league scoring the year before and, for total points for defencemen, Al Mac-Innis and Paul Reinhart had ranked third and fourth. And goalie Mike Vernon had a spectacular playoff run. As a result, most people predicted a fast start. What happened was something of a disappointment. Aside from a rousing 6-3 victory over the Oilers, there had been only three wins in the first ten games. Then they won their next seven in a row, not losing until November 18, when they faced Los Angeles. In all seven wins during the streak, Mike Vernon was in the nets. As soon as Johnson put Reggie Lemelin in against the Kings, the team lost. Back with Vernon for a couple of wins and then Lemelin for a couple of losses. The team seemed to be playing better in front of the confident young net-

minder. Gradually Vernon took over the bulk of the goaltending duties. By the end of the year, he'd played in 54 games compared to Lemelin's 34 starts. Vernon ended the season with 30 wins to Lemelin's 16, but Lemelin had a lower goals against average, 3.25 to Vernon's 3.61.

On November 12, just 16 games into the season, the Flames management made a move. They traded young centreman Dan Quinn, second in Flames' scoring the previous season, to the Pittsburgh Penguins. In exchange, they received offensive threat Mike Bullard. Wearing jersey number 25 in his

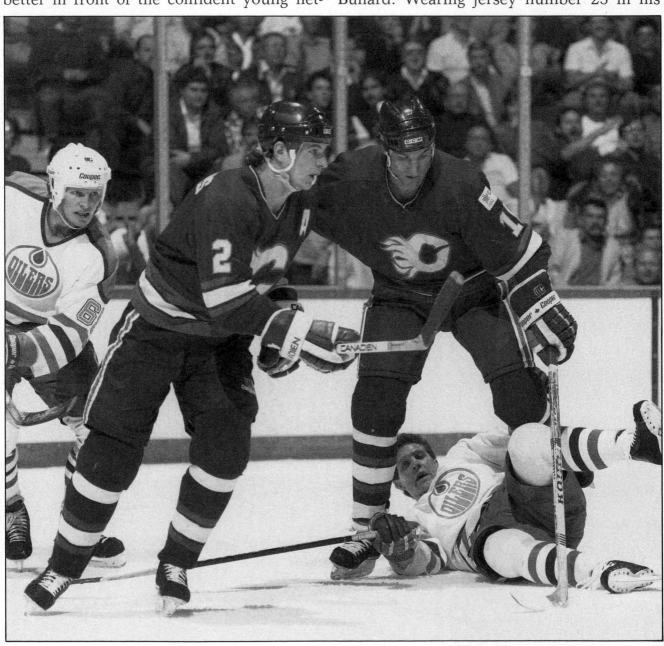

first season with the Flames, he emerged as a solid goal scorer, and a healthy addition to their power play.

In general, it was a solid season. Home and away wins were more evenly split with 25 home wins and 21 wins on the road, and their longest losing streak was four games. Joe Mullen once again led the team in offense with 47 goals and 40 assists for 87 points. Al MacInnis finished second with 76 points, followed by Paul Reinhart with 68. But the story was Joe Mullen. The deal that Cliff Fletcher had made to acquire Mullen from St. Louis stood as one of the best in franchise history. With four consecutive forty-goal seasons under his belt, and the most recent 47, it looked like a fifty-goal season wouldn't be far away.

The last week of the regular season began with Calgary on the road in Winnipeg. The Jets handed the Flames a 10-1 loss, the worst pounding the Flames had suffered in years.

Was this an omen, just before the playoffs started? A week later the season was over. Calgary finished with 95 points, six better than the previous season, and was third over-all in league standings, an increase of three places from the year before.

LEFT:

Al MacInnis and Tim Hunter. The Flames completely dominated the Oilers in the 1986-87 season, compiling a 6-1-1 record.

RIGHT:

Joe Mullen led the team in scoring in 1986-87, and won the NHL's Lady Byng Trophy, and the Molson Cup.

FOLLOWING PAGES:
Neil Sheehy and Rejean Lemelin.

ABOVE:
Mike Vernon assumed the No. 1 goaltending position in 1986 - 87, leading the team with 30 wins.

Glenn Hall, Hall of Fame goaltender and the Flames' goaltending coach, on Mike Vernon:

"I have Mike Vernon rated as the best goaltender in the NHL. His ability to be in position to stop the second shot is outstanding, and I think the best in the league. He just stands in there and takes everything thrown at him. His maturity has been his biggest asset."

OPPOSITE PAGE:
Joe "Who" Nieuwendyk, wearing jersey No. 18, played in nine games during the 1986 - 87 season. The following year, in his first full NHL season, he would switch to No. 25.

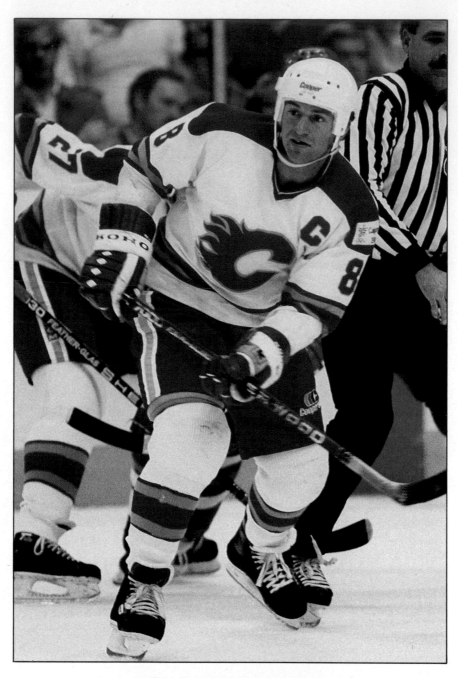

DOUG RISEBROUGH

On September 10, 1982 Calgary acquired Doug Risebrough from the Montreal Canadiens in exchange for draft picks. A key acquisition for the Flames, Doug played a total of 740 NHL games, scoring 185 goals and 286 assists for 471 points. The Flames had been working on the deal for some time and were shocked to learn of the trade between Montreal and Washington involving Rod Langway and Brian Engblom. It occurred early in the morning on the same day that the Risebrough trade was scheduled to take place. There was concern that, because of public outcry in Montreal, the trade might be in jeopardy. But it wasn't, and later that same day Risebrough was a Flame. A four-time Stanley Cup winner, Risebrough has been an important part in the overall development of the Calgary Flames. Doug Risebrough retired on June 9, 1987, and was immediately appointed an assistant coach under incoming head coach Terry Crisp.

1986 - 1987 CALGARY FLAMES

FOURTH ROW: *(left to right)* Nick Fotiu, Al MacInnis, Joe Nieuwendyk, Tim Hunter, Kevan Guy, Jamie Macoun, Neil Sheehy, Gary Roberts, Joel Otto.

THIRD ROW: Jim Peplinski (Co-Captain), Kari Eloranta. Owners: Byron Seaman, Daryl Seaman, Harley Hotchkiss, Norman Green, Norman Kwong, Sonia Scurfield. Paul Reinhart, Gary Suter, Al Murray (Assistant Trainer).

SECOND ROW: Bobby Stewart (Equipment Manager), Carey Wilson, Perry Berezan, Paul Baxter, Mike Bullard, Steve Bozek, Hakan Loob, Joe Mullen, Colin Patterson, John Tonelli, Jim Murray (Head Trainer).

FRONT ROW: Rejean Lemelin, Doug Risebrough (Co-Captain), Pierre Page (Assistant Coach), Bob Murdoch (Assistant Coach), Bob Johnson (Head Coach), Cliff Fletcher (President and General Manager), Al MacNeil (Assistant General Manager), Al Coates (Assistant to President), Lanny McDonald (Co-Captain), Mike Vernon.

ABSENT: Brian Engblom.

PLAYOFFS

Once again, Calgary would enter the playoffs like a battalion returning from a hard-fought battle. Risebrough, McDonald and Berezan were doubtful starters. Otto had been lost for the season due to knee surgery. And Hakan Loob had a broken finger. Yes, they had had Edmonton's number all season, with a 6-1-1 record. After one two-game Flames sweep, Oilers Coach Sather said, "It was like standing in the middle of a small island in the middle of the ocean and watching the tide roll in — a red tide."

But there was still one thing in the way of a Battle of Alberta rematch — the Winnipeg Jets. The Flames, by virtue of their better seasonal record, held home-ice advantage. One change from past years, though, was that the NHL had revised the semi-final playoff format from a best-of-five to a best-of-seven.

Reggie Lemelin started in goal against the Jets' Daniel "The Bandit" Berthiaume. And a bandit he proved to be as the Jets took the opener, 4-2. Coach Bob Johnson countered with Vernon for game two. The difference in this game was a disputed goal by Winnipeg's Thomas Steen scored right as the buzzer sounded to end the second period. The Jets then completely shut down Calgary in the third period. When it was over, they held a shocking two-game advantage.

Vernon started game three, and was nothing short of spectacular. Steve Bozek was back in the line-up, but Al MacInnis was out with a badly-bruised thigh. Mike Bullard popped the game winner in overtime to give Calgary win number one. The Flames were missing another key defenceman when Jamie Macoun, who was speared in the third game, was hospitalized with a severely bruised kidney and spleen. Then, early in the game, rear-guard Kevan Guy was ejected for fighting. Paul Reinhart was also injured and could play only sparingly. It ended in a 4-3 Jets victory, and a 3-1 series lead. The Flames extended the series, winning game five, 4-3. But two nights later, at the Arena in Winnipeg, the Jets eliminated the Flames, winning 6-1.

The Jets double-teamed Joe Mullen throughout the series, holding him to three points. Mike Bullard led the Flames in playoff scoring with seven points, while a new kid by the name of Joe "Who" Nieuwendyk had four. Another rookie, Brett Hull, had played well, scoring three points in the four games he played. Joe Mullen won the Molson Cup and, in June, he was named winner of the Lady Byng Trophy.

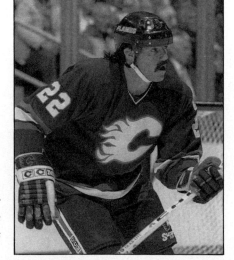

Mike Bullard was acquired in a trade with the Pittsburgh Penguins on November 12, 1986, in exchange for Dan Quinn. Bullard was Calgary's leading scorer in the playoff series against the Jets.

STATS

1986 - 87

		REGULAR SEASON						PLAYOFFS				
Coach	GP	W	L	T	PTS	GF	GA	GP	W	L	GF	GA
Bob Johnson	80	46	31	3	95	318	289	6	2	4	15	22

REGULAR SEASON HIGHLIGHTS

Most Points
JOE MULLEN 87

Most Goals
JOE MULLEN 47

Most Assists
AL MacINNIS 56

Most Penalty Minutes
TIM HUNTER 361 *

Most Wins Goalie
MIKE VERNON 30

Trophies - Awards
Lady Byng
Molson Cup
JOE MULLEN

* Flame Record

PLAYOFF HIGHLIGHTS

Most Points
MIKE BULLARD 6

Most Goals
MIKE BULLARD 4

Most Assists
GARY SUTER 3

Most Penalty Minutes
TIM HUNTER 51

Most Wins Goalie
MIKE VERNON 2

STATISTICS — REGULAR SEASON

PLAYER		GP	G	A	PTS	PIM
Joe Mullen		79	47	40	87	14
Al MacInnis		79	20	56	76	97
Paul Reinhart		76	15	53	68	22
Mike Bullard	Pit.	14	2	10	12	17
	Cal.	57	28	26	54	34
	Tot.	71	30	36	66	51
Carey Wilson		80	20	37	57	42
John Tonelli		78	20	31	51	72
Joel Otto		68	19	31	50	185
Jim Peplinski		80	18	32	50	181
Gary Suter		68	9	39	48	70
Hakan Loob		68	18	26	44	26
Jamie Macoun		79	7	33	40	111
Steve Bozek		71	17	18	35	22
Brian Bradley		40	10	18	28	16
Lanny McDonald		58	14	12	26	54
Colin Patterson		68	13	13	26	41
Tim Hunter		73	6	15	21	*361
Gary Roberts		32	5	10	15	85
Dale Degray		27	6	7	13	29
Neil Sheehy		54	4	6	10	151
Dan Quinn		16	3	6	9	14
Perry Berezan		24	5	3	8	24
Nick Fotiu		42	5	3	8	145
Kari Eloranta		13	1	6	7	9
Joe Nieuwendyk		9	5	1	6	0
Doug Risebrough		22	2	3	5	66
Kevan Guy		24	0	4	4	19
Brian Engblom		32	0	4	4	28
Paul Baxter		18	0	2	2	66
Mike Vernon		54	0	2	2	14
Brett Hull		5	1	0	1	0
Doug Dadswell		2	0	0	0	0
Rejean Lemelin		34	0	0	0	20
Totals		80	318	537	855	2018

GOALTENDERS	GP	MP	GA	AVG	W	L	T
Rejean Lemelin	34	1735	94	3.25	16	9	1
Mike Vernon	54	2957	178	3.61	30	21	1
Doug Dadswell	2	125	10	4.80	0	1	1
Totals		4817	282	3.61	46	31	3

ENG: Lemelin (4), Vernon (2), Dadswell
SO: Lemelin (2), Vernon

Joel Otto, Gary Suter and teammates protect their goal. (Inset) Jim Peplinski and Tim Hunter.

1987-88

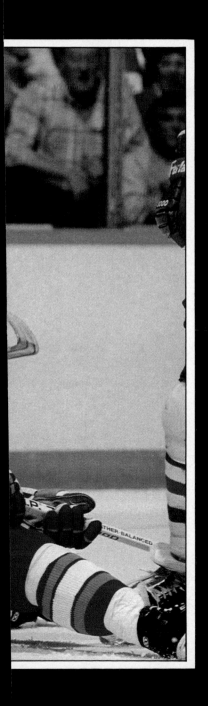

A scant five weeks after the Winnipeg Jets had ended Calgary's playoff bid in the 1986-87 season, a bombshell dropped at the Flames' offices in the confines of the Saddledome. Bob Johnson had suddenly resigned. Johnson, coach for the past five years, had accepted a job as head of the United States Amateur Hockey Association. Terry Crisp, coach for the previous two seasons with Calgary's AHL team in Moncton, was named head coach of the Flames. Bob Johnson's resignation was followed on June 4, 1987 with the announced retirement of Calgary co-captain Doug Risebrough. He was immediately named an assistant coach, along with Pierre Page who was returning for his eighth season in the Flames' organization. And Paul Baxter, who had served as both player and assistant coach under Bob Johnson, was named coach of Calgary's Salt Lake City farm team in the International League.

Early in the season, new Flames' coach Terry Crisp told his players: "I'm very abrupt. I'm abusive. I'm bellicose. I will be all over you like a blanket. I will be up and down your frame like an elevator. But please remember one thing. As long as I'm on you, I care. When you no longer hear from me, start to worry. When silence reigns supreme, look out."

In June, at the Amateur and Entry Drafts, the Flames picked 19th overall in the first round. Bryan Deasley was chosen from the University of Michigan, while another graduate of the Hull Juniors, Stephane Matteau, was chosen in the second round. It wasn't until the eighth round, 166th pick overall, that a Flames' future Stanley Cup star, Theoren Fleury, was chosen.

Just prior to the June draft, the Flames acquired veteran defenceman Ric Nattress from the St. Louis Blues for a fourth and fifth round draft choice. Two months later, on August 26, Cliff Fletcher made another important move. In exchange for a first and third round draft pick, the Philadelphia Flyers sent their defensive stalwart, Brad McCrimmon, to the Flames. McCrimmon, in company with Macoun, MacInnis, Suter,

Reinhart and Nattress, would give Calgary one of the most powerful defensive corps anywhere in the NHL.

With all the trades completed, training camp soon showed that highly-touted rookies Joe Nieuwendyk and Brett Hull would be joining the Flames' regular roster.

Slow starts to the regular season were becoming a trademark of the team, and this season would prove no different. With just two wins to show in his first seven games, new coach Terry Crisp had his work cut out for him. Crisp made the commitment before the season was two weeks old to stress defence, and to expect more of a defensive effort from his forwards. But he didn't panic. "A good plus for me is that I have Doug Risebrough as an assistant," he said. "I have Pierre Page back. I have some of Badger's

Hakan Loob had an exceptional season, leading the team in scoring with 50 goals and 56 assists for 106 points. He became the first Flame to be voted to an NHL First All-star team, and the first Swedish player to score 50 goals in a season.

notebooks, and I also have his telephone number.''

By the third week of October the Flames were back on track. Mike Vernon had become the starting goaltender and was in the nets for three consecutive wins plus a tie, and backup Doug Dadswell logged his first win of the season in a 5-3 victory over the New York Rangers. Original Calgary Flame Jim Peplinski played in his 560th game to become the club's all-time leader in that department. In late November, Calgary racked up a five-game winning streak that included a 9-1 pasting of the Quebec Nordiques. An early season three-game losing streak would be the longest of the year.

It was Calgary's Olympic year and the Flames would have to pay the price for their new arena. But just one month prior to the Flames Olympic-induced departure from the Saddledome, Cliff Fletcher traded Carey Wilson, a former star of Canada's 1985 Olympic team and defenceman Neil Sheehy to Hartford in exchange for tough right winger Shane Churla and defenceman Dana Murzyn, a Calgary native and former all-star with the WHL Wranglers.

The Saddledome would play host to a myriad of Olympic events, and between their home game against New Jersey on February 1, it would be an entire month before Calgary's next home game March 3 against Philadelphia. During this 11-game road trip, which started inauspiciously in Winnipeg with a 9-0 shutout loss to the Jets, the Flames eventually compiled a remarkable five win, five loss and one tie record. The trip was the longest in NHL history.

By the end of January, 1988, the Flames had another bona fide candidate for the Calder Trophy as Rookie-of-the-Year. Joe Nieuwendyk, who had only played nine games for Calgary the previous season and was still eligible for the award, was scoring

goals at a pace comparable to the legendary Mike Bossy in his rookie season. All at once the hockey media converged on this hot young scorer, with *Sports Illustrated*, *The Hockey News*, *The Sporting News*, and every other hockey-related magazine sending reporters and photographers to capture a part of his amazing story. He would be "Joe Who" no more. After the first 42 regular season games, Nieuwendyk had amassed an incredible 32 goals, with 19 of those coming on a fully-rejuvenated Flames power play. He would go on to have a banner season with totals of 51 goals and 41 assists for 92 points, to become only the second rookie in NHL history to reach the magic 50-goal plateau. Nieuwendyk received the coveted Calder Trophy at the end of the season, the second Flame in three years to be honoured as NHL Rookie-of-the-Year.

There were other good signs about the Flames team that year. Calgary had been neck and neck with Edmonton all year, jockeying for first place overall. Usually by mid-season the Oilers had sprinted ahead in the points race, but this year the two teams stayed within two or three points of each other, with Calgary ultimately finishing six points ahead.

On March 7, at the trading deadline, Cliff Fletcher once again made his move. Fletcher traded Brett Hull and Steve Bozek to the St. Louis Blues in exchange for veteran two-way

ABOVE:

Brad McCrimmon came from the Philadelphia Flyers in August of 1987 in exchange for a first and third round draft choice. In his first season as a Flame he won the Emery Edge Award as the league's leading plus-minus player with a plus 48, and was voted to the league's second all-star team.

RIGHT:

Brett Hull scored 26 goals in his rookie season before being traded to the St. Louis Blues with Steve Bozek for Rob Ramage and Rick Wamsley.

defenceman Rob Ramage and goaltender Rick Wamsley. Another player who joined the Flames was Czechoslovakian speedster Jiri Hrdina. He arrived after the Olympics and played in the final nine regular season games, compiling a respectable seven points. The season's disappointment was veteran defenceman Paul Reinhart whose injured back allowed him to play in only 14 games during the season. That turned the acquisition of Brad McCrimmon in the off-season into a master stroke.

At the start of the season Coach Crisp had asked his team to play a more defensive style and by the year-end it was evident that head way had been made. The Flames compiled a 48-win, 23-loss and 9-tie season, their best ever, capturing first place overall in the league. They had popped in a team record of

397 goals for, and 305 against. The prestigious Presidents' Trophy was Calgary's for the first time in team history. It was truly something to celebrate.

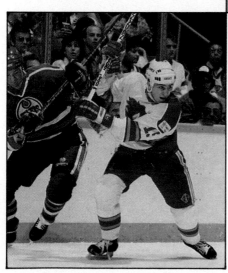

ABOVE:
Solid stay-at-home defenceman Ric Nattress was acquired from the St. Louis Blues at the start of the season.

CENTRE:
Defenceman Dana Murzyn, a native Calgarian, came from Hartford.

LEFT:
Rugged right winger Shane Churla also came from Hartford.

101

In Winnipeg, on November 10, 1987, original Calgary Flame Jim Peplinski played in his 560th NHL game, becoming the all-time team leader in games played.

"Jim Peplinski plays hockey like a cymbal clash and leads like Winston Churchill. He wins on the theory of irresistable force dominating the immovable object and has been the heart of the Flames for years."

Stan Fischler

Joe Nieuwendyk had a phenomenal rookie season. Scoring 51 goals and 41 assists for 92 points, he became only the second rookie in NHL history to reach the magic 50-goal plateau. Nieuwendyk won the coveted Calder Trophy as Rookie-of-the-Year.

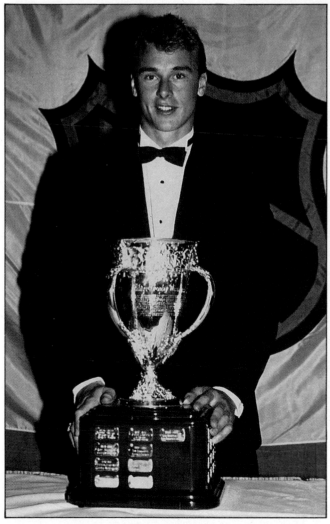

Goaltender Rick Wamsley was a standout for Montreal and St. Louis before coming to the Flames.

Rob Ramage, an experienced two-way defenceman, was acquired with Wamsley in a trade from St. Louis.

Co-captain Jim Peplinski was loaned to the Canadian Olympic Team for the 1988 Winter Games. He played in seven games as left winger for the national squad.

Right winger Hakan Loob had a banner year in 1986-87, winning the Molson Cup and being selected a first team all-star. Loob had 50 goals and 56 assists for 106 points.

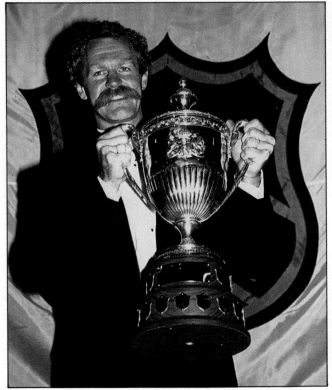

Lanny McDonald was the inaugural winner of the NHL's King Clancy Memorial Award for commitment and service to hockey.

Czech player Jiri Hrdina joined the Flames shortly after the Calgary Winter Olympics.

1987 - 88 CALGARY FLAMES

FOURTH ROW: Jamie Macoun, Joe Nieuwendyk, Rob Ramage, Joel Otto, Brian Glynn, Craig Coxe, Dana Murzyn, Ric Nattress, Gary Roberts.

THIRD ROW: John Tonelli, Perry Berezan, Gary Suter. Owners: Byron Seaman, Norman Kwong, Norman Green, Harley Hotchkiss, (Clare Rhyasen, VP Business & Finance), Sonia Scurfield. Shane Churla, Colin Patterson, Al MacInnis, Al Murray (Assistant Trainer).

SECOND ROW: Bobby Stewart (Equipment Manager), Paul Reinhart, Rick Wamsley, Brad McCrimmon, Mike Bullard, Hakan Loob, Joe Mullen, Jiri Hrdina, Tim Hunter (Alternate Captain), Jim Murray (Trainer).

FIRST ROW: Doug Dadswell, Jim Peplinski (Co-Captain), Doug Risebrough (Assistant Coach), Pierre Page (Assistant Coach), Terry Crisp (Head Coach), Cliff Fletcher (President and General Manager), Al MacNeil (Assistant General Manager), Al Coates (Assistant to President), Lanny McDonald (Co-Captain), Mike Vernon.

ABSENT: Daryl Seaman (Owner).

PLAYOFFS

Calgary opened the playoffs against fourth-place Los Angeles. Mike Vernon started in goal for the series with the Kings, and by all indications after game one — a 9-2 drubbing by Calgary — the series wouldn't last long. And it didn't. Calgary won the second game 6-4. Returning to Los Angeles, the Kings responded in the third game with a 5-2 win, their only victory of the series. In the fourth game, Calgary dominated with a 7-3 win, and then ended the Kings' season two nights later back at the Saddledome with a solid 6-4 win.

With the preliminaries over, it was now on to the series everyone was waiting for — The Battle of Alberta. The Oilers had dismissed the Jets in similar fashion to the Flames' disposal of the Kings, and the stage was set with Calgary holding home ice advantage. However, it was almost over before it started. As Mike Vernon would later say: ''Every time I looked up I saw Wayne Gretzky, Jari Kurri or Mark Messier coming in on me. I've played a lot of hockey against the Oilers over the years. But I've never seen the big guys playing better.''

Edmonton's four-game sweep over the regular season champion Flames was a total and utter shock. ''Of all the years I've been here,'' said Wayne Gretzky, ''I don't think I've ever seen our team really bear down and prepare as strongly as it did for this series.'' The Flames were shut down. Although they averaged 4.9 goals per game during the regular season, against the Oilers they were held to an average of 2.75 goals per game. During the regular season, Calgary's potent power play had converted 28.5 percent of its chances, but against Edmonton in the Smythe Division final they only scored four times on 27 power play opportunities. As Lanny McDonald said, ''They played more desperately than we did. You have to give them full marks for the kind of effort they put in.'' It was all over so fast.

STATS

1987 - 88

Coach	REGULAR SEASON							PLAYOFFS				
	GP	W	L	T	PTS	GF	GA	GP	W	L	GF	GA
Terry Crisp	80	48	23	9	105	397	305	9	4	5	41	36

REGULAR SEASON HIGHLIGHTS

Most Points
HAKAN LOOB 106
Most Goals
JOE NIEUWENDYK 51
Most Assists
GARY SUTER 70
Most Penalty Minutes
TIM HUNTER 337
Most Wins Goalie
MIKE VERNON 39
Calder
JOE NIEUWENDYK
King Clancy
LANNY McDONALD
Emery Edge
BRAD McCRIMMON
All-Star
HAKAN LOOB 1st - RW
BRAD McCRIMMON 2nd - Defence
GARY SUTER 2nd - Defence

PLAYOFF HIGHLIGHTS

Most Points
GARY SUTER 10

Most Goals
HAKAN LOOB 8

Most Assists
GARY SUTER 9

Most Penalty Minutes
JIM PEPLINSKI 45

Most Wins Goalie
MIKE VERNON 4

OPPOSITE PAGE: *Brad McCrimmon and Lanny McDonald protect their goal.*

STATISTICS — REGULAR SEASON

PLAYER		GP	G	A	PTS	PIM
Hakan Loob		80	50	56	106	47
Mike Bullard		79	48	55	103	68
Joe Nieuwendyk		75	51	41	92	23
Gary Suter		75	21	70	91	126
Joe Mullen		80	40	45	85	30
Al MacInnis		80	25	58	83	116
John Tonelli		74	17	41	58	82
Joel Otto		62	13	40	53	192
Jim Peplinski		75	20	31	51	234
Brett Hull		52	26	24	50	12
Rob Ramage	ST.L.	67	8	34	42	127
	Cal.	12	1	6	7	37
	Tot.	79	9	40	49	164
Brad McCrimmon		80	7	35	42	100
Carey Wilson		34	9	21	30	18
Gary Roberts		74	13	15	28	282
Lanny McDonald		60	10	13	23	57
Craig Coxe	Van.	64	5	12	17	186
	Cal.	7	2	3	5	32
	Tot.	71	7	15	22	218
Perry Berezan		29	7	12	19	66
Brian Glynn		67	5	14	19	87
Colin Patterson		39	7	11	18	31
Dana Murzyn	Har.	33	1	6	7	45
	Cal.	41	6	5	11	92
	Tot.	74	7	11	18	137
Ric Nattress		63	2	13	15	37
Tim Hunter		68	8	5	13	337
Steve Bozek		26	3	7	10	12
Neil Sheehy		36	2	6	8	73
Jiri Hrdina		9	2	5	7	2
Mike Vernon		64	0	7	7	47
Shane Churla	Har.	2	0	0	0	14
	Cal.	29	1	5	6	133
	Tot.	31	1	5	6	147
Paul Reinhart		14	0	3	3	10
Kevan Guy		11	0	3	3	8
Doug Dadswell		25	0	2	2	2
Rich Chernomaz		2	1	0	1	0
Randy Bucyk		2	0	0	0	0
Bob Bodak		3	0	0	0	22
Rick Wamsley	ST.L.	31	0	0	0	14
	Cal.	2	0	0	0	0
	Tot.	33	0	0	0	14
Totals		80	397	652	1049	2429

GOALTENDERS		GP	MP	GA	AVG	W	L	T
R. Wamsley	ST.L.	31	1818	103	3.40	13	16	1
	Cal	2	73	5	4.11	1	0	0
	Tot.	33	1891	108	3.43	14	16	1
Mike Vernon		64	3565	210	3.53	39	16	1
Doug Dadswell		25	1221	89	4.37	8	7	2
Totals			4859	304	3.75	48	23	9

ENG: Vernon (1)
SO: Vernon (1)

[Inset] Al MacInnis and the Conn Smythe Trophy.

1988-89

*T*he previous year's playoffs had seen a shocking turn of events. After finishing first overall in the league, and beating Edmonton four games to three in the regular season, the Flames had gone down in four straight games to the Oilers in the second round. It would make for a long summer for both the team and its fans. And the annual June entry draft wasn't expected to be a highlight either as the Flames, by virtue of their league-leading regular season performance, would receive the 21st, and last, pick in the first round. They chose Jason Muzzatti, a goaltender from Michigan State, as their first choice, and Todd Harkins, a six foot three inch right winger, for their second round pick. Then, in the 12th round, the 252nd pick overall, Cliff Fletcher took a shot in the dark and chose Sergei Priakin, a twenty-five-year-old left winger from the USSR. Many NHL clubs made a habit of choosing Russian players in the later rounds just in the hopes that something might come of it in later years, so not much interest was given to Fletcher's choice.

Although it was a quiet summer as far as news about the team went, a major trade was announced one week prior to the start of training camp. Mike Bullard, a recent Flame who had arrived in 1986 in a trade with Pittsburgh for Dan Quinn, had enjoyed a good regular season in 1987-88. Bullard was second in Flames' scoring with 48 goals and 55 assists for 103 points, just three behind leader Hakan Loob. But in the playoffs, playing two games against Los Angeles in the first round and all four against the Oilers in the second, he contributed a total of two assists. His disappointing playoff performance set Cliff Fletcher looking for a trade, and on September 5, in a deal that would have significant bearing on the Flames' Stanley Cup victory, a major trade was announced. Bullard, along with Tim Corkery and Craig Coxe, would report to the St. Louis Blues in exchange for Doug Gilmour, Mark Hunter, Steve Bozek and Michael Dark. But Bozek,

the ex-Flame, didn't last long in Calgary as he was soon traded, along with Paul Reinhart, to Vancouver for future draft picks.

Jiri Hrdina, the Czech acquired just after the Olympic Games, got off to a fast start. He scored a hat trick against Los Angeles on October 17, and then had a four-goal game against the Whalers at the Saddledome on November 7. Hrdina had become a fixture on the power-play along with Joe Nieuwendyk and Hakan Loob. By early December, after playing 22 games, he had 12 goals and 13 assists and was second only to Joe Sakic of the Nordiques in rookie scoring.

The team was also off to a fast start and, on November 23, after defeating the visiting New Jersey Devils, the Flames moved into first place overall in the league. Coach Crisp had once again started the season by trying to convince his players to sacrifice personal goals for the good of team defence. Once more, the team responded. At this point in the season the club had given up the fewest goals in the league and goaltenders Vernon and Wamsley had the first and third-best goals against averages in the league. On De-

Mike Bullard

Mark Hunter

Doug Gilmour

cember 8, with a 5-3 win over the Oilers, the Flames extended their unbeaten streak to 13 games, a club record. And a week later, they would set another record: seventeen straight games undefeated on home ice. The return of Jamie Macoun from an off-season car accident had bolstered the defence, and their offence had been strengthened by the acquisitions of Gilmour and Hunter from St. Louis. "Our team is three players better than last year," said Cliff Fletcher. "There is no doubt in my mind that on paper, and so far on the ice, this is our best team ever." The Flames' record had proven his words. After 28 games into the season, Calgary had only lost four games, and three of those four games were one-goal losses.

Just three days into the New Year, in a game against Quebec, Flames fans were treated to something they hadn't seen before, and certainly weren't expecting. Theoren Fleury had been called up from the Salt Lake Golden Eagles. In 40 games with the Golden Eagles, Fleury had scored 37 goals and added 37 assists to earn a shot with the Flames. Against the Nordiques, he hit everything in

sight. Against Los Angeles two nights later he recorded three assists. But the real thrill for him and his growing legion of fans would come on January 7th against Edmonton when he scored two goals in a 7-2 Flames' victory. A love affair had begun. At five feet six inches and 155 pounds, Fleury was one of the smallest, and one of the most exciting, players in the NHL.

BELOW:
Lanny McDonald scores his 490th career goal on November 23, 1988 helping the Flames take over first place in the league. He is congratulated (left) by his teammates.

In February, 1989, four Calgary Flames — Joe Mullen, Gary Suter, Joe Nieuwendyk and Mike Vernon — were selected to travel to Edmonton for the 40th annual All-Star game. Mike Vernon emerged as the winning goalie and Joe Mullen was just edged out of the MVP honours, and a new car, by Wayne Gretzky.

Mike Vernon had earned his spot on the All-Star roster by compiling an impressive goals against average of 2.71. Earlier in the season he had put together a 12-game unbeaten streak and followed that up in January and February with a 13-game winning streak. During the 1988-89 season Vernon played in a total of 52 games, ending the year with his best ever average of 2.65. He set a club record for goaltenders with 37 wins, 6 losses, and 5 ties. Rick Wamsley, who played in 35 games, ended with a 2.96 average on his way to compiling a record of 17 wins, 9 losses and 1 tie.

Defenceman Gary Suter would find 1988-89 to be his toughest year as a pro. After missing only a single game all year, on February 22, after an appendectomy, he was sidelined for a further 16 games. Suter's point total fell to 62 from the previous season high of 92. Newcomer Mark Hunter also had injury problems and lost a total of ten games due to a separated shoulder and a concussion. But the team, overall, had given Coach Terry Crisp everything he had asked for at training camp, and more. A club record year-end low of 226 goals against was an incredible 79 goals lower than the previous year. And a club record high of 54 victories enabled them to join a most elite club — that of NHL teams who have won 50 or more games in one season. Only Montreal, Boston, Philadelphia and Edmonton had ever accomplished that. Calgary's longest losing

Jamie Macoun was solid on defence.

streak of the season was only two games. Most importantly, they had beaten the Montreal Canadiens for first place overall in the league — their second Presidents' Trophy in two years — and they would have home-ice advantage throughout the playoffs.

Before the playoffs started, however, Cliff Fletcher had two more moves to make. On March 4, just before the trading deadline, he moved Perry Berezan and Shane Churla to the North Stars in exchange for Brian MacLellan and a fourth round draft pick. He also sent the Flames' Director of Public Relations, Rick Skaggs, to Toronto. Just the Toronto Airport, actually, to pick up Sergei Priakin and return home to Calgary with him safely in hand. Negotiations had been going on between the Calgary President/General Manager and the Soviet Ice Hockey Federation since January, and the deal was struck on March 25 in Toronto. On March 31, against the Winnipeg Jets at home in the Saddledome, Priakin played in his first NHL game. Two days later he suited up against the Oilers in the last game of the regular season. After watching Priakin — whom he had drafted in the 12th round, 252nd overall, in the 1988 entry draft — Fletcher said, "His hockey sense and anticipation look good. He's going to be an effective NHLer."

On December 23, the flu bug hit Joe Mullen, sidelining him for one game. But for No. 7, it was the only blemish on an otherwise perfect season. Mullen led the Flames with 51 goals and 59 assists for 110 points. He also led Calgary in the plus-minus category with an incredible plus 51. And he capped off a dream season by setting a new mark in total points scored by an American-born player. As well, he contributed seven game-winning goals, second only to the 11 game-winning goals that Joe Nieuwendyk scored. Centre Joe Nieuwendyk also scored 51 goals, the second year in a row that he hit the 50 goal mark, and ended the season in third place in team scoring with 82 points. This was the first time in Calgary Flames history that they would have two 50-goal scorers on their roster in one year.

As good a season as Vernon, Mullen and Nieuwendyk had, it was Lanny McDonald's year. After 15 seasons in the league, starting with the Toronto Maple Leafs, then the Colorado Rockies, and finally the Flames, he was approaching two of hockey's most elusive milestones. On March 7, 1989, at the Saddledome against the Winnipeg Jets, he ripped a slapshot from the top of the face-off circle that eluded Jets goalie Bob Essensa and found the back of the net. Lanny McDonald had scored his 1000th NHL point. This, his 5th goal of the season, came at 2:46

Jiri Hrdina and Craig McTavish battle at centre ice during a game between the Flames and Oilers on December 8, 1988. The Flames won, extending their unbeaten streak to 13 games.

of the first period, with assists to Hrdina and Murzyn. At 3:17 of the third period, he did it again, scoring his 6th season goal and his 1001st point. McDonald received two standings ovations that night as the Flames went on to beat the visiting Jets 9-5.

Two weeks later, on March 21 in a game against the visiting New York Islanders, it would be vintage McDonald again. His classic wrap-around effort fooled Islanders goalie Mark Fitzpatrick, and McDonald had achieved his second milestone—his 500th NHL goal. A late-season spurt of seven goals in seven games had warranted Coach Crisp to give McDonald more and more ice time. Dressing for only 51 games during the year, he compiled 11 goals and 7 assists for 18 points. As McDonald chipped away at those two awesome milestones, and the number of games left dwindled, it became the main topic of conversation. His teammates and coaches had no doubt about him achieving the 500-goal mark. Before skating out onto the ice for the game against the Islanders, McDonald decided to wear one of his Legend T-Shirts. After scoring his 500th goal he wore the shirt in every game. Said McDonald: "It's hard to describe. As soon as it happened, it was the most peaceful feeling ever."

All in all, it had been the best regular season ever for the Calgary Flames.

ABOVE:
Joe Nieuwendyk makes Flames history against Winnipeg on January 11, 1989, by scoring five goals in one game.
LEFT:
Theoren Fleury, in his second NHL game, had three assists.
OPPOSITE PAGE: *"Rick Wamsley (31) is a valuable asset to this club and is the ultimate team player."*   Glenn Hall

1989 ALL-STARS

The 1989 All-Star Game featured four Flames: (l to r)
Joe Mullen, Joe Nieuwendyk, Mike Vernon, Gary Suter.

*Just before the March, 1989 trading deadline Cliff Fletcher traded veteran
Perry Berezan (above right) and Shane Churla to the Minnesota North Stars
for rugged left winger Brian MacLellan (above left), and a fourth round pick.*

*In Montreal, Joe Mullen receives the 1989 Emery Edge
Award from Gordie Howe. Mullen had the league's best
plus-minus rating with an incredible plus 51.*

*The Flames acquired another international player when
Sergei Priakin, their 12th round pick from the 1988 Entry
Draft, came from the Soviet Wings on March 29.*

CAPPING AN INCREDIBLE SEASON

Joe Mullen, Lanny McDonald, and Joe Nieuwendyk display the pucks that kept going in, and in, and in. Mullen (left) and Nieuwendyk (right) both reached the magic 50-goal plateau (the first time the Flames have had two 50-goal scorers in one season), while McDonald (centre) recorded both his 500th career goal and his 1000th career point.

SMYTHE DIVISION SEMI-FINAL
CALGARY vs. VANCOUVER

Calgary was the runaway leader in the Smythe Division, finishing 26 points ahead of the second place Los Angeles Kings, 33 points ahead of the Oilers, and 43 points ahead of the Vancouver Canucks. The first round of the playoffs against the Canucks would be sandwiched between two exciting overtime games. In the opening game of the series, the Flames came out flat and found themselves facing sudden-death overtime. Paul Reinhart, the former Flame now starring with Vancouver, scored from the slot to give Vancouver the win.

For the Flames, Game Two couldn't come soon enough. Aching for a chance to redeem themselves, they gave up four power plays to the Canucks in the first period. But it was how they played in those short handed situations that turned the game in their favour. After Joel Otto connected for a short handed goal the Canucks were on the run. Goals by Patterson, Fleury, Gilmour and Loob led the Flames to a 5-2 win, and evened the series at one game apiece.

Games Three and Four were held in Vancouver, and though Vancouver came on strong in Game Three, the Flames weathered an early storm, and Mike Vernon held them off the scoreboard. Vernon recorded his first shutout of the playoffs and Loob, with two, plus singles by Mullen and Nieuwendyk, secured the Flames win. In the first three games, the Flames penalty killing had been excellent, holding the Canucks to only one power play goal in 22 opportunities.

But the Canucks rebounded in Game Four with a 5-3 win and it was back to the Saddledome for Game Five with the series tied at two games each.

Game Five was almost an exact repeat of Game Three in that the Flames received goals from Mullen, Nieuwendyk, and Loob, plus a goal by Mark Hunter as Vernon posted his second shutout of the playoffs, again by a 4-0 score. But it wasn't all happiness after the game as the Flames learned that their all-star defenceman and former Calder Trophy winner Gary Suter was gone for the rest of the playoffs, the victim of a broken jaw received from the elbow of Vancouver's Mel Bridgman.

Back in Vancouver for Game Six, Mike Vernon faced a barrage of shots from an inspired Canucks' team, and the Flames could not put them away. Garth Butcher scored the winner for Vancouver as the Canucks posted a 6-3 victory, forcing a seventh and deciding game to be played in Calgary.

Former Flame Paul Reinhart scores in overtime during the first game of the first round of the playoffs.

Joe Nieuwendyk opened the scoring at the nine-minute mark of the first period, but three minutes later Robert Nordmark tied it up for the Canucks. Gary Roberts scored at the end of the period, but just two minutes into the second period Vancouver's Trevor Linden tied it at 2-2. The score stayed tied during a back and forth second period until Joe Mullen popped one in during the last minute of play, giving the Flames a 3-2 lead. In the third, Calgary couldn't get the puck past Kirk McLean in the Vancouver nets for the insurance goal, and at the 7:12 mark Doug Lidster scored, tying the game at three. Calgary was unable to respond with the go-ahead, and once more they were headed into overtime.

It was a fast, furious, and absolutely heart-stopping overtime period. At one end of the rink McLean made a spectacular save off a rushing Joe Mullen, while at the other end, Mike Vernon stretched to get the glove on a Stan Smyl slapshot one minute and a slider by Petri Skriko the next. Both goalies were unbeatable until, with only 39 seconds left in the first overtime period, Joel Otto deflected a pass from Jim Peplinski to give the Flames a 4-3 victory—and the march was on to the Stanley Cup! The Vancouver series was as close a call as the Flames could ever want. Mike Vernon, with his stellar 45 save performance, was the game's first star, while Joel Otto was second. Kirk McLean, who had stopped literally one shot less than Vernon, was the third star.

That same night Wayne Gretzky and the Los Angeles Kings eliminated the Oilers in the other Smythe Division semi-final match, and the next round matchup was finally set.

ABOVE:

Mike Vernon celebrates the dramatic Game Seven over-time victory over Vancouver that helped carry the Flames on the road to the Stanley Cup.

OPPOSITE PAGE:

Coach Terry Crisp and the Flames' bench celebrate Doug Gilmour's overtime goal in game one vs. Los Angeles.

SMYTHE DIVISION FINAL
CALGARY vs. LOS ANGELES

DANNY RIEDLHUBER, CALGARY SUN

The first game of the Calgary — Los Angeles series went according to the pundit's script: a high scoring, end-to-end game that was as different as night and day from the close-checking Vancouver series. Theoren Fleury opened the scoring late in the first period, only to have Bernie Nicholls even it up two minutes later. In the second period, the Kings newly-acquired Chris Kontos scored early, then MacLellan tied it up again for the Flames. But just before the second period ended Weimer scored on Vernon with a blast from just inside the point and the period ended with the Kings in front 3-2. Calgary battled to come back and with just 1:36 left in the third, Gary Roberts scored on a pass from Dana Murzyn to force Calgary's third overtime game in only eight playoff games. At 7:47 of overtime, Doug Gilmour freed the puck from Marty McSorley and slipped it past Hrudey to give the Flames the win. In-including the regular season, it was the fifth straight loss in the Saddledome for the Kings.

Game Two was almost over before it got started. Fifty-eight seconds into the game, Colin Patterson scored off a Dana Murzyn pass. Four minutes later, Doug Gilmour scored from McDonald, and two minutes later Gilmour scored again. And then, in one of the most unusual goals in NHL history, Al MacInnis scored with assists to Loob and Nieuwendyk and Bearcat Murray. In a goal-mouth scramble, Nicholls had decked Vernon with a haymaker, and as the Flames carried the puck down the ice towards Hrudey, Bearcat jumped onto the ice and ran to help a fallen Vernon. The Kings, seeing the trainer on the ice, let up just enough to allow Mac-Innis to walk in alone and blast one into the net. The goal was allowed to stand, and basically the game was over as Calgary went on to win 8-3.

"We set the tone early," said Lanny Mc-Donald. "The two overtime games really gave us confidence. It gave us a chance to build on something. You do what you have to do. You find ways to win. That's the most relaxed, confident game we've played." In that game, Calgary had 52 shots on goal, a new club record.

Game Three in Los Angeles saw Mike Vernon remain virtually unbeatable as the Flames won their third in a row with a 5-2 victory. With an off-day the next day, some

Joel Otto tests Kelly Hrudey.
Coach Crisp about Joel Otto:
"There's a fire that burns inside him and it's the same sort of fire that burns inside every leader."

Mark Hunter, who had his wrist injured in the Vancouver series, gets his skates done up by Al Murray. Hunter came back to play in the last games of the Stanley Cup final.

Joe Mullen, with Joel Otto right beside him, bears down on Hrudey, as Doug Gilmour looks for the rebound.

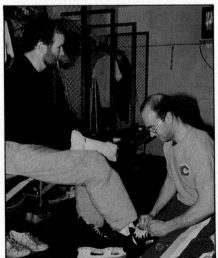

Gary Roberts and Jim Weimer entangled over a sprawlen Kings goalie Kelly Hrudey.

of the Calgary players went to the Dodgers baseball game and some to the ocean, but most stayed put at the hotel and relaxed at the pool. After the scare of the Vancouver series, this was not the time to celebrate. It was the time to concentrate on putting the Kings away in the fourth game and winning the series.

But it would not be an auspicious start to Game Four. The Kings controlled both the play and the puck for the early going with Nicholls scoring first. Joe Mullen brought the Flames back into the game with a power-play goal, followed by a goal by Gary Roberts a minute later. And just before the end of the period, Los Angeles tied it up. The second period was tighter defensively, with only Joe Nieuwendyk scoring at the 19-minute

mark. Early in the third, Joe Mullen scored again, but the Kings closed to within one, and then were forced to pull their goalie in favour of an extra attacker. Gary Roberts shot into an empty net to score and clinch the series victory for Calgary. The Flames had held the Kings — the highest scoring team in the NHL — to just 11 goals, and had swept them in four straight games.

Said Bernie Nicholls after the loss: "Their big guys didn't take any bad penalties, they played with a tremendous amount of discipline. I really think we had the talent to win, but they are a great hockey team."

Two nights later, the Chicago Black Hawks defeated the St. Louis Blues to win their series four games to one. The next round was set.

"Our defence feels better than a year ago. The turning point for us was the Vancouver series; they prepared us for L.A. Our defensive hockey was back. We had to take away the middle on them. We stood them up at the blue line, the guys held them down. We plugged up the centre of the ice, the place the goalscorers like to play."

Mike Vernon, after the L.A. series

CAMPBELL CONFERENCE FINAL
CALGARY vs. CHICAGO

It was almost impossible to know what to expect. Calgary had played Chicago three times during the regular season, and had beaten them each time. But Chicago had come on late in the season and had been doing well so far in the playoffs. Although it had taken an overtime goal in the last game of the regular season to defeat Toronto just to get into the playoffs, they had defeated both the Detroit Red Wings and the St. Louis Blues easily in the first two playoff rounds.

The first game started cautiously for both teams, but Jamie Macoun, on a blast at 10:08, put the Flames on the board. Midway into the second period Nieuwendyk scored on a power play to make it 2-0, and then MacLellan scored in the third to put the game away. The Flames had easily handled Chicago and Mike Vernon had his third shutout of the playoffs — after having gone the entire season without a single one! Said Chicago Coach Mike Keenan: "There's not much to say. We just got the crap beat out of us."

Game Two was a total reversal. Six minutes into the game the shots on goal were nine for Chicago and none for Calgary. And on the scoreboard it was 3-0 for Chicago. Although Loob and Mullen would score for the Flames, it was Chicago's game and they won it 4-2.

Game Three was held at the Chicago Stadium, the NHL's loudest arena, where every visiting team wants to score first to take the crowd out of the game for the Hawks. It took red-hot Joe Mullen just four minutes to score Calgary's first goal, and Joe Nieuwendyk backed him up with another goal ten minutes later. Chicago came back early in the second, but Theoren Fleury scored to put the Flames ahead 3-1. Chicago answered late in the period to set the scene for the final twenty minutes. It was all Calgary in the third, as Hakan Loob scored his 9th playoff goal and Joe Mullen followed with his 11th as Calgary beat the Black Hawks 5-2.

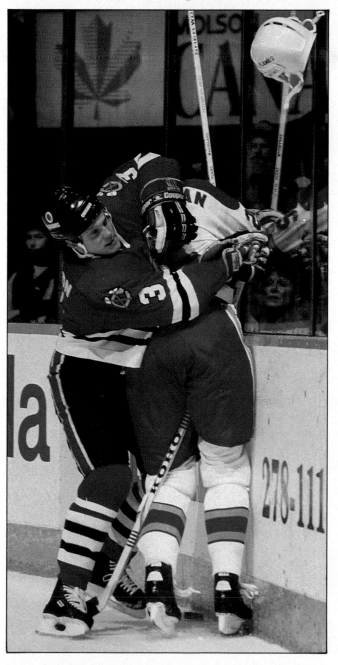

Chicago's Dave Manson barely escapes an elbowing penalty on Calgary's Brian MacLellan as they meet behind the net in Game One of the series.

"If we stay with the mature part of the game, not taking retaliatory penalties, we'll do alright."

Coach Terry Crisp

While most players used the day off between games to relax and renew their energies, that wasn't the case for Colin Patterson. Early the next morning Patterson boarded a plane back home to Calgary. He had just heard—four hours after the victory in Chicago—that he had become the father of a baby girl, and he rushed home to spend what was left of the off-day with his wife Sherry and his new daughter. Five hours before Game Four he arrived back in Chicago with the first pictures of Stephanie Grace Patterson.

Game Four in Chicago saw the Black Hawks come out aggressively and they had an early power play. The Flames held them off with their tenacious forechecking, and the first period ended scoreless, although Calgary was ahead 12 to 3 in shots.

In the middle of the second, with Joel Otto off on a five minute major and Rob Ramage off for two minutes, Chicago opened the scoring. At the 18:03 mark of the second period Doug Gilmour scored from MacInnis and Fleury on the power play to even the score. It had been Calgary's first shot on goal in a full 13 minutes of play. Both teams had their opportunities to score in the third but both goaltenders were unbeatable. This would be Calgary's fourth overtime game in the playoffs. The last time these two teams had gone into overtime in the playoffs was in 1981 when Willi Plett scored to win the game and the series for the Flames. In the 1989 rematch, MacLellan had an opportunity to tip in the winner off a point shot from Mac-Innis, but Chevrier made the save. Calgary then was forced to kill a penalty, a rare occurrence in overtime. This would be Chicago's 27th power play opportunity in the series, and they had only scored once. The Flames had proved themselves to be masters at killing penalties. Then, at 13:47 of the overtime, Trent Yawney of the Hawks took a two minute minor penalty for delay of game and, just before his penalty expired, Al Mac-Innis blasted a shot from inside the blueline off a pass from Fleury to end the game. Coach Crisp jumped the glass behind Calgary's bench to give Norma MacNeil a kiss while the bench exalted in the victory. The Flames were taking a 3-1 series lead back home.

Game Five was Joe Nieuwendyk's game. The Flames, led by Nieuwendyk, held a 1-0 lead after the first period. Late in the second Chicago scored after killing a five minute major and a game misconduct by Creighton.

Lanny McDonald squeezes past Steve Konroyd of Chicago.

Jamie Macoun and Colin Patterson team up on the boards.

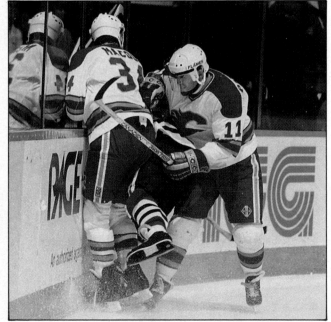

The score was tied 1-1, and it came down to a twenty minute game for the Campbell Conference Championship. At 5:19 of the third MacLellan deflected a point shot by Ric Nattress to give the Flames a one goal lead. Then, at 16:59, Joe Nieuwendyk scored his second of the game to clinch a 3-1 victory at the Saddledome.

Joe Mullen described the play of his teammate Joe Nieuwendyk: "What did you ex-pect from him? This is playoff hockey. You give what you've got, and Joe's got a lot to give. Tonight you saw another example of his character, of how he cares."

After a quick raise of the Campbell Conference Bowl to the crowd, the team left the ice. "There's a bigger, better Cup out there," said Lanny McDonald. And it was on to the Stanley Cup finals!

The Campbell Conference Bowl is presented to Co-Captains Tim Hunter, Lanny McDonald and Jim Peplinski.

STANLEY CUP FINALS
CALGARY vs MONTREAL
GAME ONE

Al MacInnis on the Flames' fans:

"The fans were great. The whole city is behind us. The way they give us the ovations at the start of the games, we were really pumped. The fans are great."

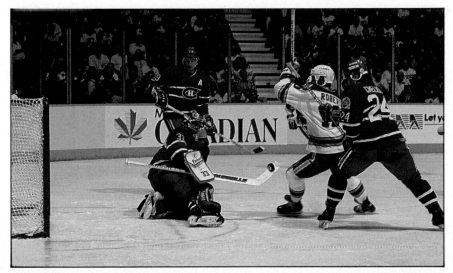

Gary Roberts, with Chris Chelios in hot pursuit, almost scores on Patrick Roy.

The game-plan was simple. Hold the Canadiens for the first five minutes, let Calgary's tenacious forechecking close down the ice, wait for your chances, and see what happens. On paper, the Flames had more offence. They were also very successful checkers, and had ranked second overall in the league in fewest goals against. Hold them for five minutes. Yes, it was a good plan, but at 2:43 of the first period Stephane Richer found the net on a power play and Montreal was ahead. Three minutes later, it was Calgary's turn on the power play and Al MacInnis blasted one in from Mullen and Otto and the game was tied. Two minutes later, MacInnis scored again, followed by Robinson for Montreal and the first period ended in a tie. Theoren Fleury came up big at 11:45 of the second period to score what proved to be the game winner, assisted by Jamie Macoun and Tim Hunter. Calgary showed they could protect a lead and Game One was Calgary's—their 10th in their last 11 playoff games.

GAME TWO

Game Two was, as dozens of newspaper articles and television and radio commentaries expounded, crucial. Statistics said that the winner of Game Two would be the team that would take home the Cup. Three years earlier, Montreal had won Game Two in overtime in Calgary and gone on to win the next three. But this year's team was different. ''First of all,'' said Lanny McDonald, ''We're three years older, three years wiser and a heck of a lot stronger as a team.''

Montreal came out strong with goals by Larry Robinson in the first period, and Bobby Smith early in the second. The Flames came back to dominate the period, outshooting the Canadiens by a 16 to 4 margin, and tied it up on goals by Joe Nieuwendyk and Joel Otto. But in the third period, although the shots were equal at eight apiece, Chelios and Courtnall scored to give the Canadiens a 4-2 victory. With the series tied at one, the two teams packed up and headed east to the Forum in Montreal.

Patrick Roy feels the heat from the Flames attackers.

Tim Hunter introduces himself to Patrick Roy.

GAME THREE

Having lost Game Two in the Saddledome, Game Three now became the crucial game. Once again Calgary would try to check the Canadiens into the ice for the first five or so minutes of the game and once again the Canadiens would score first. This time it was a Mike McPhee shot at only 1:32 of the first period. Joe Mullen countered with his 12th of the playoffs late in the period, with assists to McCrimmon and Gilmour. Mullen scored again late in the second, assisted by MacInnis and Fleury, an assist which extended MacInnis' playoff scoring streak to 13 games. Bobby Smith tied the game at 1:36 of the third, but Doug Gilmour put the Flames ahead again on a goal assisted by Tim Hunter. And then the roof fell in. With Patrick Roy pulled from the Canadiens net for an extra attacker, the Canadiens rallied to tie the game at 19:19 on a goal by Mats Naslund. At the end of regulation time, the Flames had outshot Montreal 28 to 17, but Patrick Roy had been the difference.

The Canadiens dominated the first overtime period, outshooting Calgary 12 to 5, but this time Mike Vernon was the difference. During the second overtime period the teams began to tighten up defensively

Joe Mullen scores his 12th playoff goal.

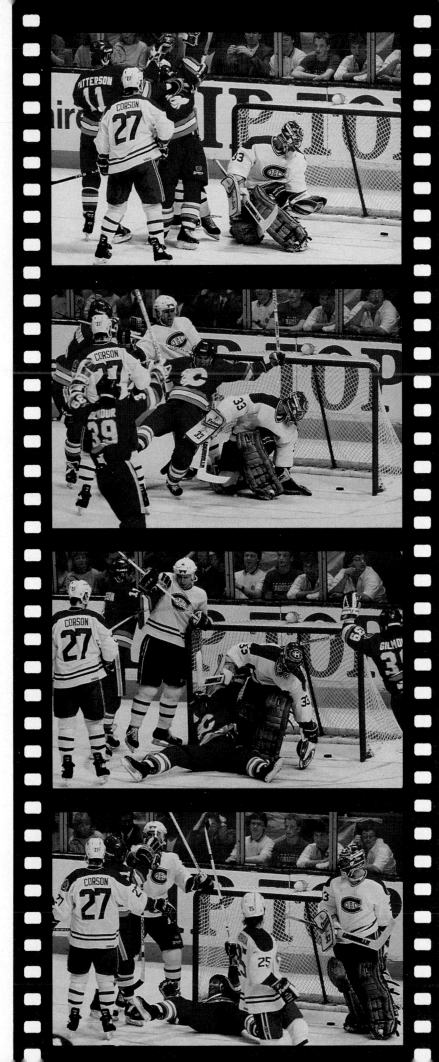

Calgary's bench rises after the Flames score in game three in Montreal.

and there were few scoring opportunities. It was past midnight in Montreal when, at 16:08 of what was officially the fifth period of the game, Calgary's Mark Hunter was sent to the penalty box on a boarding call. Exactly two minutes later at 18:08, before Hunter had time to get back into the play, Ryan Walter slipped the puck between Mike Vernon's legs and one of the longest final round overtime games in NHL history was over. Montreal, by virtue of their 4-3 win, was now in command of the series. Controversy raged in the press for the next two days over the penalty call, but for the Flames the game was over. Game Four was all that mattered, and now it was a live or die situation.

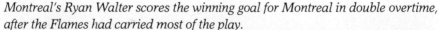

Montreal's Ryan Walter scores the winning goal for Montreal in double overtime, after the Flames had carried most of the play.

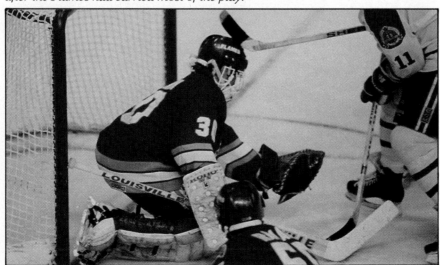

GAME FOUR

It was showtime, alright.

"Time to show what we're made of," said Al MacInnis. "To show what got us here. To show how much we want the Cup."

There was no question about it. With the Canadiens enjoying a 2-1 lead in the series, and Game Four on Forum ice, the Stanley Cup wouldn't be won on this night, but it certainly could be lost if Calgary didn't win. It was without a doubt one of the most important games in franchise history. Coming off the double overtime loss two nights before, all eyes were on the Flames. It was gut-check time. As Ric Nattress said, "I don't like to call it a do-or-die game because a team needs four to win, but I guess you might refer to it as a do-or-you're-gonna-die game."

In order to win, the Flames had to accomplish two things. Firstly, they had to hold off the Canadiens attack for the first five minutes, and secondly, they had to score first. Up to this point in the series they had been unable to accomplish either one. Consequently, they were down two games to one and facing a repeat of the 1986 playoffs.

As the first period unfolded the Flames dominated the Canadiens and only the goal-tending of Patrick Roy, who faced 13 shots, kept the Canadiens in the game and the first period ended scoreless. In the second, the Canadiens were able to generate more offense but it was the Flames who did the scoring. Doug Gilmour scored unassisted at the 11:56 mark, followed by Joe Mullen at 18:43, with assists to Al MacInnis and Joel Otto. Midway through the third, Russ Courtnall put the Canadiens on the board with his 8th playoff goal. The score remained 2-1 for the Flames until the 18:22 mark when Al MacInnis scored, appearing to put the game away. But less than a minute later Claude Lemieux put Montreal back in the game scoring on a pass from Larry Robinson, who was playing in his 201st career playoff game. But the feisty Lemieux was called for a slashing penalty after the goal, and though the goal would stand, Calgary would go on the power play. Joe Mullen, with his 15th goal of the play-offs, scored just sixteen seconds into the power play, with assists from Doug Gilmour and Colin Patterson. With their 4-2 victory, Calgary had split their games in the Forum and the series was even again at two games each.

Patterson (left) celebrates as Mullen scores to tie the series.

135

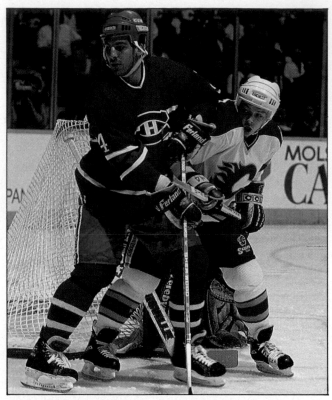

Theoren Fleury gets into position while Chris Chelios attempts to tie him up.

Red-hot playoff scorer Joe Mullen hovers on Patrick Roy's crease looking for a rebound.

The Flames returned home right after Game Four, arriving at the International Airport in the wee hours of the morning. A light practice was scheduled for 4:30 that afternoon.

The next evening, it was a delirious Game Five Saddledome crowd that watched as Joel Otto took the opening faceoff, skated in on Patrick Roy, shot, and then deflected his own rebound into the net just 28 seconds into the game. The assists went to Jim Peplinski and Mark Hunter. Joe Mullen followed with his 16th goal of the playoffs, from Gilmour and Ramage. The Canadiens fought back to within one on a Bobby Smith goal at the 13:24 mark, but Al MacInnis closed out the first period with a goal of his own, from Ramage and Joel Otto, and the first period ended with the Flames ahead 3-1.

Just past the midway point of the second period Montreal scored to close the gap to one, but Mike Vernon shut them out the rest of the way, proving again that the Flames were more than capable of protecting a one-goal lead. As Rob Ramage said, "It's trench warfare out there. You're out there in the pits, just trying to survive." But survive they had, and now they had a commanding three games to two lead in the series—one game away from the Cup!

But still they weren't celebrating. As Doug Gilmour said, "We have to play Game Four all over again. We're too far away to start thinking we can taste it now. There's no point thinking like that. We have to play scared. We have to go in there and be afraid to lose."

GAME SIX

"There isn't a guy in this room that isn't at an emotional peak. Everyone is just working so hard. You look around this dressing room at the exhaustion and how spent everyone is but every night someone digs down and comes to the fore."

Rob Ramage

The Canadiens, after losing Game Five in Calgary, flew directly home immediately after the game. The Flames chose to stay the night in Calgary, practising on home ice early the next morning, then taking the noon flight to Montreal. It was drizzling rain as their charter pulled out on the tarmac. Their last sight of Calgary was of the airport ground crew standing in the rain on the side of the runway waving GO FLAMES GO! signs as the charter taxied out.

Montreal was hot and muggy again. And at the game day practice at the Montreal Forum the press was everywhere. News had broken of the Russians releasing Sergei Makarov, and the reporters besieged Cliff Fletcher. As well, preparations were underway for the Stanley Cup presentation should the Flames be the first team in NHL history to be presented with the Cup on Montreal ice. Through all this, the players went about their game day workout.

Across the rink, the Canadiens' dressing room was quiet. Their players dressed quickly and left the building. They wanted to be alone, away from the reporters and news media and their probing questions. During the regular season, the line of Carbonneau, Corson and Naslund had combined for 85 goals. But in the five games played so far in this final series, they had clicked for only one. The Calgary defence had been tenacious. Carbonneau had been held pointless, and Corson had only one assist. Calgary's magic line of Gilmour, Mullen and Patterson had combined speed and offense with a grinding style of checking. During the regular season, Mullen had led the league with a plus 51. Gilmour was a plus 45 while Patterson came in at a plus 44, for an incredible total of plus 140. The Canadiens had countered against them with Carbonneau, Gainey and Keane, but it had not been effective. Add to that the fact that Mike Vernon had played brilliantly,

ABOVE: *Lanny McDonald scored his first-ever NHL goal in the Montreal Forum. On this night, sixteen years later, he scored his last. His wife, Ardell, was in attendance at the Forum on both occasions.*

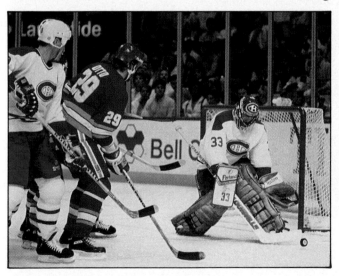

LEFT: *Roy stops the ever-pressing Joel Otto in close.*

137

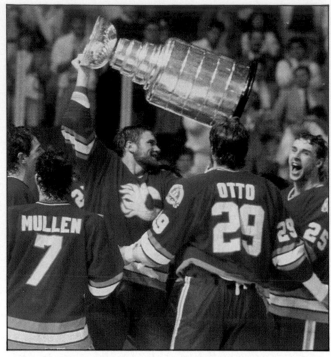

A joyous celebration as the Flames break a 68-year-old tradition by winning the Stanley Cup on Montreal's ice!

and that Al MacInnis had been virtually unstoppable. This night, all of the pressure would be on the Canadiens. '

Adding to the sense of anticipation in the air was the arrival at 1:30 in the afternoon of the players' wives from Calgary, as well as the presence of all six owners of the Flames. And to top it all off, both Ric Nattress and Rick Wamsley were celebrating birthdays.

During the pre-game warm-up, Assistant Coach Tom Watt layed out his case and Coach Terry Crisp concurred. Lanny Mc—Donald would play in Game Six. And they

would stick to the same game plan they had used throughout the series. Firstly, don't take dumb, retaliatory penalties. Secondly, hold Montreal's attack in the opening minutes. Thirdly, score first.

After only fifty-four seconds into the game, Joe Mullen was sitting in the penalty box. The Flames killed it. Montreal continued throughout the first period to mount a sustained attack, but Vernon held solid. Then, at the 18:51 mark, Colin Patterson shot from the top of the circle and popped it past Roy, with assists to Dana Murzyn and Al MacInnis. The period ended with the Flames up 1-0. MacInnis, with his last assist, had now registered a point in 17 consecutive playoff games, an NHL record for defencemen.

Claude Lemieux evened up the score at 1:23 into the second period, but just three minutes later, at 4:24, Lanny McDonald stepped out of the penalty box, took a pass and skated in on the right wing. He lifted the puck over Roy's left shoulder and Calgary had taken the lead again. Assists went to Joe Nieuwendyk and Hakan Loob.

Play was even in the third period, with Mike Vernon ignoring a couple of stiff checks and holding Montreal off the scoreboard. At 11:02, Doug Gilmour scored Calgary's third goal which appeared to have put the game away. But almost before the goal, with assists to Otto and Al MacInnis, was announced, Rick Green had brought the Habs back to within one. The Canadiens pressed, but Calgary held. Then Doug Gilmour got free and scored his second of the period, with assists from Mullen and Macoun. Roy was pulled a few seconds later but the Flames defence held the fort. Calgary had won the game 4-2 and the final series 4-2. The Stanley Cup was theirs!

At centre ice, NHL President John Ziegler presented the Cup to Lanny McDonald, Jim Peplinski and Tim Hunter. Al MacInnis was rewarded for his outstanding play by winning the Conn Smythe Trophy as Most Valuable Player during the playoffs.

The dressing room was pandemonium. If there had been ten Stanley Cups to hold and drink out of—there still wouldn't have been enough to go around. Everyone wanted to get their hands on the Cup. And not one Flame player had ever won it before. For Lanny, it

ABOVE:
Gary Roberts (l) and Dana Murzyn.

LEFT:
Bearcat Murray and Ric Nattress.

RIGHT:
Joel Otto.

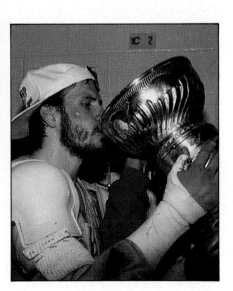

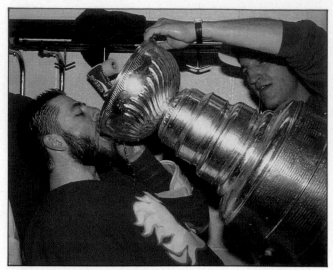

Brad MacCrimmon and Tim Hunter

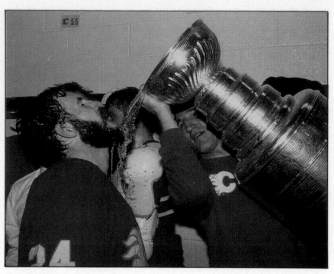

Jamie Macoun

had been a 16-year wait. For Theoren Fleury, only a five-month wait. For the owners, it had been nine years. But everyone had their chance to sip champagne from the Cup.

Montreal Coach Pat Burns summed it up best. "The difference was that they were able to score on their chances and we weren't. They played with revenge. Losing that Cup in the 1986 playoffs obviously hurt a lot. They didn't want to go through it again."

In taking the Cup on this night, the Calgary Flames had broken a 68-year tradition of the Montreal Canadiens by winning it on their home ice. Lanny McDonald was quick to note that he had scored his first NHL goal on Forum ice when he was with the Maple Leafs, and he had ironically scored his last

NHL goal in the same building. And both times his wife had been in the stands!

In the dressing room, eight weeks growth of beards disappeared. On the streets of Calgary, thousands celebrated through the night. Plans were being made for a victory parade through downtown Calgary. It was 1:30 a.m. Calgary time when the Flames finally reached Mirabel Airport in Montreal to begin the ride home. A four-hour party at forty thousand feet was in full swing as the Stanley Cup Champions headed west across Ontario, Manitoba, Saskatchewan, and finally, at 5:00 in the morning, arriving home in Calgary. Jubilation reigned. The Stanley Cup, the Conn Smythe Trophy, and the Calgary Flames were home. Champions!

Doug and Marilyn Risebrough

Gary and Cathy Suter

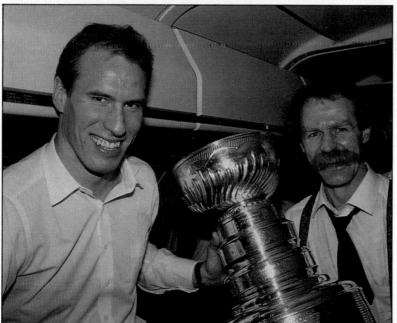

ABOVE:
Sheila and Terry Crisp

ABOVE LEFT:
Al Coates and Paul Baxter

LEFT:
Jim Peplinski and Lanny McDonald

BELOW:
The owners of the Calgary Flames celebrate on the charter plane home:

(Clockwise) Harley Hotchkiss, Norman Kwong, Daryl (Doc) Seaman, Byron Seaman, Norman Green, and Sonia Scurfield.

Al MacInnis won the Conn Smythe Trophy as the Most Valuable Player in the Stanley Cup playoffs. He led all players in total points scored with 7 goals and 23 assists for 30 points. MacInnis also scored at least one point in seventeen consecutive games to establish an NHL playoff record for defencemen.

1989 STANLEY CUP CHAMPIONS

FOURTH ROW: Rob Ramage, Joe Nieuwendyk, Sergei Priakin, Dana Murzyn, Joel Otto, Brian MacLellan, Ric Nattress, Mark Hunter.

THIRD ROW: Al Murray (Assistant Trainer), Gary Roberts, Jamie Macoun. Owners: Daryl Seaman, Harley Hotchkiss, Byron Seaman, Sonia Scurfield, Norman Kwong, Norman Green. Theoren Fleury, Jiri Hrdina, Jim Murray (Trainer).

SECOND ROW: Bobby Stewart (Equipment Manager), Allan MacInnis, Colin Patterson, Brad McCrimmon, Hakan Loob, Joe Mullen, Doug Gilmour, Gary Suter, Tim Hunter (Co-Captain), Glenn Hall (Goaltending Coach).

FRONT ROW: Rick Wamsley, Jim Peplinski (Co-Captain), Tom Watt (Assistant Coach), Doug Risebrough (Assistant Coach), Terry Crisp (Head Coach), Cliff Fletcher (President and General Manager), Al MacNeil (Assistant General Manager), Al Coates (Assistant to President), Lanny McDonald (Co-Captain), Mike Vernon.

STATS
1988-89

STANLEY CUP CHAMPIONS

REGULAR SEASON HIGHLIGHTS

Most Points
JOE MULLEN 110

Most Goals
JOE MULLEN, JOE NIEUWENDYK 51

Most Assists
DOUG GILMOUR, JOE MULLEN 59

Most Penalty Minutes
TIM HUNTER 375

Most Wins Goalie
MIKE VERNON 37

Trophies - Awards - All-Stars
JOE MULLEN RW 1st
AL MacINNIS DEF 2nd
MIKE VERNON GOAL 2nd

Molson Cup, Lady Byng Trophy
JOE MULLEN

PLAYOFF HIGHLIGHTS

Most Points
AL MacINNIS 31

Most Goals
JOE MULLEN 16

Most Assists
AL MacINNIS 24

Most Penalty Minutes
JIM PEPLINSKI 75

Most Wins Goalie
MIKE VERNON 16

Conn Smythe Trophy
AL MacINNIS

STATISTICS — REGULAR SEASON

PLAYER		GP	G	A	PTS	PIM
Joe Mullen		79	51	59	110	16
Hakan Loob		79	27	58	85	44
Doug Gilmour		72	26	59	85	44
Joe Nieuwendyk		77	51	31	82	40
Al MacInnis		79	16	58	74	126
Gary Suter		63	13	49	62	78
Jiri Hrdina		70	22	32	54	26
Joel Otto		72	23	30	53	213
Brian MacLellan	Min.	60	16	23	39	104
	Cal.	12	2	3	5	14
	Tot.	72	18	26	44	118
Gary Roberts		71	22	16	38	250
Colin Patterson		74	14	24	38	56
Jim Peplinski		79	13	25	38	241
Theoren Fleury		36	14	20	34	46
Mark Hunter		66	22	8	30	194
Jamie Macoun		72	8	19	27	76
Brad McCrimmon		72	5	17	22	96
Dana Murzyn		63	3	19	22	142
Lanny McDonald		51	11	7	18	26
Rob Ramage		68	3	13	16	156
Tim Hunter		75	3	9	12	375
Ric Nattress		38	1	8	9	47
Mike Vernon		52	0	4	4	18
Rick Lessard		6	0	1	1	2
Ken Sabourin		6	0	1	1	26
Brian Glynn		9	0	1	1	19
Steve Guenette	Pit.	11	0	1	1	0
	Cal.	0	0	0	0	0
	Tot.	11	0	1	1	0
Rick Wamsley		35	0	1	1	8
Rich Chernomaz		1	0	0	0	0
Stu Grimson		1	0	0	0	5
Sergei Priakin		2	0	0	0	2
Dave Reierson		2	0	0	0	2
Paul Ranheim		5	0	0	0	0
Totals		80	366	596	962	2492

GOALTENDERS	GP	MP	GA	AVG	W	L	T
Mike Vernon	52	2938	130	2.65	37	6	5
Rick Wamsley	35	1927	95	2.96	17	11	4
Totals	80	4871	225	2.78	54	17	9

SO: Wamsley 2